# Lecture Notes in Artificial Ii

## Subseries of Lecture Notes in Computer Science

### LNAI Series Editors

Randy Goebel
  *University of Alberta, Edmonton, Canada*
Yuzuru Tanaka
  *Hokkaido University, Sapporo, Japan*
Wolfgang Wahlster
  *DFKI and Saarland University, Saarbrücken, Germany*

### LNAI Founding Series Editor

Joerg Siekmann
  *DFKI and Saarland University, Saarbrücken, Germany*

Stephen Cranefield   Insu Song (Eds.)

# Agent Based Simulation for a Sustainable Society and Multi-agent Smart Computing

International Workshops, PRIMA 2011
Wollongong, Australia, November 14, 2011
Revised Selected Papers

 Springer

Series Editors

Randy Goebel, University of Alberta, Edmonton, Canada
Jörg Siekmann, University of Saarland, Saarbrücken, Germany
Wolfgang Wahlster, DFKI and University of Saarland, Saarbrücken, Germany

Volume Editors

Stephen Cranefield
University of Otago
Department of Information Science
P.O. Box 56, Dunedin 9054, New Zealand
E-mail: scranefield@infoscience.otago.ac.nz

Insu Song
James Cook University
School of Business/IT, Australia
1 James Cook Drive, Douglas, QLD 4811, Australia
E-mail: insu.song@jcu.edu.au

ISSN 0302-9743          e-ISSN 1611-3349
ISBN 978-3-642-35611-7    e-ISBN 978-3-642-35612-4
DOI 10.1007/978-3-642-35612-4
Springer Heidelberg Dordrecht London New York

Library of Congress Control Number: Applied for

CR Subject Classification (1998): I.2.11, I.6.3, I.6.5-7, K.4.4, J.2, K.4.1, J.7

LNCS Sublibrary: SL 7 – Artificial Intelligence

*Typesetting:* Camera-ready by author, data conversion by Scientific Publishing Services, Chennai, India

Printed on acid-free paper

Springer is part of Springer Science+Business Media (www.springer.com)

# Preface

This volume contains selected and revised versions of papers that were presented at two of the workshops held at the 14th International Conference on Principles and Practice of Multi-Agent Systems (PRIMA 2011) on November 14, 2011, in Wollongong, Australia. PRIMA is one of the oldest active agent computing forums, beginning in 1998 as a regional agent workshop (the Pacific Rim International Workshop on Multi-Agents).

Alongside the main conference, PRIMA includes workshops that are intended to facilitate active exchange, interaction and comparison of approaches, methods and various ideas in specific areas related to intelligent agent systems and multi-agent systems. In alignment with the conference theme for PRIMA 2011 of "Agents for Sustainability," the 2011 workshop program sought to encourage thought leadership in the agent community as to how agent computing can be applied to enhance sustainable practices in our world, from agriculture and personal resource usage to the design and operation of more sustainable cities. The call for workshops invited proposals for workshops addressing this theme, as well as workshops that continued to explore the "Agents and Services" theme of PRIMA 2010, which addressed connections to service science and service-oriented computing.

The two workshops covered by this volume are the Workshop on Agent-Based Simulation for a Sustainable Society (ABSSS 2011) and the International Workshop on Multi-Agent Smart Computing (MASmart 2011). A third workshop was also held at PRIMA 2011: the Second International Workshop on Services and Agents (ServAgents 2011).

Papers submitted to these workshops were reviewed by at least two reviewers, and the accepted papers were included in the informal workshop proceedings and presented at the workshops. Selected papers were then invited to be revised and submitted for consideration for inclusion in this volume after further review by the workshop Program Chairs.

The PRIMA 2011 workshops were held at the University of Wollongong, Australia, which provided generous support. Particular mention goes to the conference General Chairs, Aditya Ghose and Guido Governatori, the Local Organizing Chairs, Minjie Zhang and Hoa Dam, the ServAgent 2011 Organising Committee (Hoa Khanh Dam and Aditya Ghose), the ABSSS 2011 Organising Committee (Frank Dignum, Virginia Dignum, Liz Sonenberg, Yoshi Kashima and Sarah Hickmott), and the MASmart 2011 Organizing Committee (Takayuki Ito and Gokiso Showa-ku). Finally, we thank the members of the workshop Program Committees who produced timely reviews under time constraints.

July 2012                                                    Stephen Cranefield
                                                             Insu Song

# Organisation

## Programme Committees

### ABSSS

| | |
|---|---|
| Frank Dignum | Utrecht University, The Netherlands |
| Virginia Dignum | Delft University of Technology, The Netherlands |
| Alexis Drogoul | IRD, UPMC, MSI-IFI, Vietnam |
| Bruce Edmonds | Manchester Metropolitan University, UK |
| Benoit Gaudou | University of Toulouse, France |
| Hiromitsu Hattori | Kyoto University, Japan |
| Ho Tuong Vinh | UMI UMMISCO, IRD, IFI, Vietnam |
| Peter McBurney | Kings College, London, UK |
| Yuu Nakajima | Kyoto University, Japan |
| Craig Pearson | University of Melbourne, Australia |
| Jens Pfau | University of Melbourne, Australia |
| Dirk van Rooy | Australian National University, Australia |
| David Scerri | RMIT University, Australia |
| Alex Smajgl | CSIRO, Australia |
| Liz Sonenberg | University of Melbourne, Australia |
| Tiberiu Stratulat | Polytech Montpellier, France |
| Sung-Bae Cho | Yonsei University, South Korea |
| Patrick Taillandier | University of Toulouse, France |
| The Duy Bui | Vietnam National University, Vietnam |

### MASmart

| | |
|---|---|
| Takayuki Ito | Nagoya Institute of Technology, Japan |
| Tokuro Matsuo | Yamagata University, Japan |
| Minjie Zhang | University of Wollongong, Australia |
| Shohei Kato | Nagoya Institute of Technology, Japan |
| Akira Iwata | Nagoya Institute of Technology, Japan |
| Naoki Fukuta | Shizuoka University, Japan |
| Ivan Marsa-Maestre | University of Alcala, Spain |
| Miguel A. Lopez-Carmona | University of Alcala, Spain |

## Workshop Organisers

### ABSSS

| | |
|---|---|
| Frank Dignum | Utrecht University, The Netherlands |
| Virginia Dignum | Delft University of Technology, The Netherlands |
| Liz Sonenberg | University of Melbourne, Australia |
| Yoshi Kashima | University of Melbourne, Australia |
| Sarah Hickmott | RMIT University, Australia |

## MASmart

| | |
|---|---|
| Takayuki Ito | Nagoya Institute of Technology, Japan |
| Tokuro Matsuo | Yamagata University, Japan |
| Minjie Zhang | University of Wollongong, Australia |
| Shohei Kato | Nagoya Institute of Technology, Japan |
| Akira Iwata | Nagoya Institute of Technology, Japan |
| Naoki Fukuta | Shizuoka University, Japan |
| Ivan Marsa-Maestre | University of Alcala, Spain |
| Miguel A. Lopez-Carmona | University of Alcala, Spain |

## PRIMA Workshop Chairs

| | |
|---|---|
| Stephen Cranefield | University of Otago, New Zealand |
| Insu Song | James Cook University, Australia |

# Table of Contents

# Multi-Agent-Based Simulation for Analysis of Transport Policy and Infrastructure Measures

Johan Holmgren[1], Linda Ramstedt[2], Paul Davidsson[3], and Jan A. Persson[3]

[1] School of Computing, Blekinge Institute of Technology, SE-374 24 Karlshamn, Sweden
johan.holmgren@bth.se
[2] Vectura, Svetsarvägen 24, SE-171 11 Solna, Sweden
linda.ramstedt@vectura.se
[3] School of Technology, Malmö University, SE-205 06 Malmö, Sweden
{paul.davidsson,jan.a.persson}@mah.se

**Abstract.** In this paper we elaborate on the usage of multi-agent-based simulation (MABS) for quantitative impact assessment of transport policy and infrastructure measures. We provide a general discussion on how to use MABS for freight transport analysis, focusing on issues related to input data management, validation and verification, calibration, output data analysis, and generalization of results. The discussion is built around an agent-based transport chain simulation tool called TAPAS (Transportation And Production Agent-based Simulator) and a simulation study concerning a transport chain around the Southern Baltic Sea.

**Keywords:** Multi-agent-based simulation, MABS, Multi-agent systems, Supply chain simulation, Freight transportation, Transport policy assessment.

## 1 Introduction

Freight transportation causes different types of positive and negative effects on the society. Positive effects typically relate to economy and social welfare, e.g., due to the possibility to consume products that have been produced far away. Negative effects mainly relate to the environment, and typical examples are emissions, congestion and energy use. Public authorities in the role of policy makers often have a wish to reach certain governmental goals, such as obtaining sustainable transport systems and meeting emission targets. A typical ambition of a public authority is to increase the internalization of external costs, e.g., by letting road users pay for the road wear they cause [1]. However, internalization of external costs may have effects that might be negative on other goals. For instance, it might lead to negative economic development in a region. For enterprises, the goal is typically to maximize profit, e.g., through optimization of their activities (either individually or in collaboration), by reducing lead-times, lowering transport costs, improving delivery accuracy, etc.

By applying different types of transport policy and infrastructure measures, hereafter referred to as transport measures, it is often possible for public authorities and corporate decision makers to influence how transports are carried out. However, it is important to be able to accurately predict what the consequences will be when applying transport measures, so that undesired effects can be avoided and desired effects can be confirmed.

S. Cranefield and I. Song (Eds.): PRIMA 2011 Workshops, LNAI 7580, pp. 1–15, 2012.

Essentially, there are three types of transport measures that are relevant to apply to a transport system:

1. Control policies including different types of taxes and fees, such as kilometer and fuel taxes, and regulations, such as weight restrictions on vehicles.
2. Infrastructure investments in roads, railway tracks, intermodal freight terminals, industry tracks, etc.
3. Strategic business measures, such as improvement of timetables and adjustment of vehicle fleets to better meet the transport demand.

Multi-agent-based simulation (MABS) is able to model the actual complexity of a transport system, e.g., by explicitly modeling decisions of different actors (e.g., transport operators and transport buyers), their interaction, time aspects (including timetables and time-differentiated taxes and fees), etc. This is necessary to get accurate results when assessing the impact of transport measures, and it makes MABS more powerful than traditional approaches to transport analysis, such as SAMGODS [19,3], SMILE [20] and TRANS-TOOLS [15]. Whereas traditional approaches rely on assumed statistical correlation between different parameters, MABS relies on causality, i.e., decisions and negotiations determine how transport activities are performed. Since MABS is able to capture the interaction between actors, as well as their heterogeneity and decision making, it enables more explicit modeling of the complex multi-actor processes involved in finding and agreeing upon transport solutions. Typical questions that can be studied using MABS models for impact assessment of transport measures include:

– Which logistical effects (e.g., concerning transport route/mode choices, order sizes and order frequencies) will appear in a particular transport network under the influence of a set of transport measures.
– How will the costs and quality of service (e.g., possible delays) change as a consequence of the introduction of a set of transport measures.
– What will the environmental impact (e.g., $CO_2$ emissions) be when introducing a set of transport measures?

The purpose of this paper is to elaborate on the usage of MABS for impact assessment of transport policy and infrastructure measures (transport measures). We build our discussion around experiences that we have gained when developing and using an agent-based simulation tool called TAPAS (Transportation And Production Agent-based Simulator) [2]. We briefly describe TAPAS, as well as a simulation study that has been conducted with TAPAS. The simulation study concerns transportation in a transport corridor around the Southern Baltic Sea.

In our work we focus on the TAPAS simulation tool even though there exist several other MABS models that can be used for assessing the impact of different types of transport measures, e.g., provided by Gambardella et al. [6] and Liedtke [14]. We assume that they in most aspects concerning how to conduct simulation studies are similar, even though they are different in many other aspects.

By presenting and accounting for how to conduct a MABS study for impact assessment of transport measures, we contribute with respect to determining the purpose of a study, designing simulation experiments, validating scenarios, and analyzing simulation results including the possibility of obtaining generalizable results. Particular aspects that are addressed in the discussion are our experiences concerning participatory and collaborative modeling and simulation, how to select which entities and aspects to include in a simulation study, and how multi-criteria analysis with MABS can be used when analyzing the impact of transport measures, e.g., to assess whether measures are good enough from a sustainability perspective. We believe that our work may be valuable when developing new MABS models for impact assessment of transport measures, and when designing and conducting simulation studies using existing models.

In the next section we give an overview of TAPAS, followed in Section 3 by a description of a simulation study that has been conducted with TAPAS. Section 4 contains our main contribution, which is a discussion on how to design and conduct simulation studies with MABS models, and in Section 5 we provide some concluding remarks.

## 2   The TAPAS Simulation Tool

We here briefly describe the TAPAS simulation model, which is an agent-based tool for simulation of decision making and activities in transport chains. The main purpose of TAPAS is to function as a decision support system for different types of users and stakeholders by allowing them to study different types of transport measures. A detailed description of TAPAS, including technical details, is provided in [8].

As illustrated in Fig. 1, TAPAS makes use of a 2-tier architecture including a physical simulator and a decision making simulator. The physical simulator models all physical entities (e.g., links, vehicles, and products) and their activities, and in the decision making simulator, six transport chain decision makers (or roles) are modeled as agents.

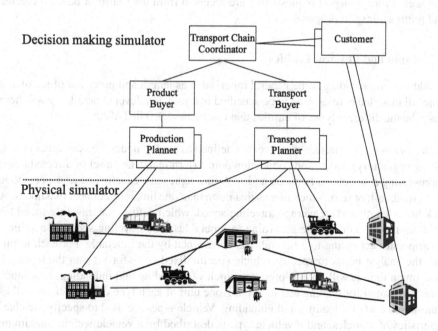

**Fig. 1.** Architectural overview of the TAPAS simulation model

## 2.1  Decision Makers and Their Interaction

To fulfill a customer demand, the agents participate in a process that includes ordering of products and a transport solution, selection of which resources and infrastructure to use, and planning of how to use resources and infrastructure. The process starts when a customer sends an order request to the transport chain coordinator, and it ends when products and a transport plan have been booked and confirmed.

The *customer* is responsible for ordering products in quantities that keep customer inventories at levels that minimize the costs for inventory holding and ordering (order cost includes costs for production and transportation) while reducing the risk of running out of stock. The *transport chain coordinator* is responsible for fulfilling customer orders by requesting products from the product buyer and transport solutions from the transport buyer. For a number of candidate order quantities, it finds the best combination of products and transportation and lets the customer determine which quantity should be delivered. The *product buyer* is responsible for finding products in order to satisfy product requests (from the transport chain coordinator), and it communicates with the production planners by sending product requests and receiving product proposals. A *production planner* is responsible for planning the production in a producer node, based on available production resources and costs. Production costs and times when products can be picked-up are sent to the production buyer as a response to a product request, and production planners are also responsible for sending bookings to the factories. The *transport buyer* is responsible for combining transport proposals that are received from the transport planners into producer-to-customer transport solutions. Each *transport planner* controls a fleet of vehicles, which operates in some geographical area. From transport requests that are received from the transport buyer it creates and returns transport proposals.

## 2.2  Input and Physical Entities

In addition to providing some general input, such as length and precision of simulated time, all modeled entities need to be specified in a sufficient level of detail. We will here describe the different types of entities that can be modeled in TAPAS.

*Transportation.* The transport network is defined as a set of nodes, i.e., customer nodes, producer (factory) nodes, and connection points (terminals), and a set of directed links, representing connections between nodes. A link represents exactly one transport mode (e.g., road, rail, or sea), which means that more than one link may connect two nodes. A link has a length and an average traveling speed, which defines the traveling speed for vehicles that do not operate according to timetables. The traveling speed of a vehicle that operates according to a timetable is determined by the timetable. For each terminal, the analyst needs to specify vehicle-specific fixed costs for visiting the terminal, how much time it will take to prepare vehicles for loading and unloading, how much time is required for loading and unloading one unit of each type of product, as well as time-based costs for loading and unloading. Vehicle types are used to specify the characteristics of vehicles, and a vehicle type is described by a vehicle weight, maximum allowed weight (including load), load capacity (i.e., a set of storages with capacities), fuel (or energy) type, distance-based fuel consumption, emissions (e.g., $CO_2$ and $NO_x$) per unit of consumed fuel, and transport mode. A fuel type (e.g., diesel or electricity) is defined by a cost and a tax that is charged per unit (e.g., liter or kWh). Four types of transport cost components can be defined; time-based costs (e.g., driver and deterioration of products), distance-based costs (e.g., fuel, vehicle wear, and kilometer tax), link-based costs (e.g., road tolls), and fixed operator-based ordering costs (e.g., administration). TAPAS provides two approaches for determining the price for buying transport capacity. In one approach, the price depends linearly on the size of the order, based on assumed average load utilization for the particular type of transport. In the other approach, a risk cost is added to cover for uncertainties regarding future bookings.

*Storage.* Storages are defined for vehicles, and for customer and producer nodes. A storage type is described by the types of products that can be stored, and whether or not multiple product types can be stored simultaneously. For example, it might be possible to store more than one type of liquid in the same tank, but not at the same time. A storage is described by a storage type, additional restrictions regarding which product types can be stored (other than specified for the particular storage type), as well as capacity (weight and volume). Moreover, it is possible to specify time-based costs for storing products, which are differentiated on product type and storage owner.

*Production and Consumption.* A product type is described by mass and volume attributes, and for each product type that can be produced in a producer node, the following parameters should be specified: cost for raw material (for the particular node), maximum batch size, batch production time, batch setup time, and time-based production cost. The price for products is the cost for raw material plus the production cost, which is proportional to the production time. Even though batch production is assumed, the parameters that describe production can be adjusted to represent: (1) batch production, (2) continuous production, and (3) instant retrieval of products from storage (however without considering inventory costs for the products). Moreover, for each type of product that can be consumed in a customer node, the analyst needs to define several types of parameters describing the ordering behavior, e.g., maximum allowed inventory level, safety-stock level, and estimated (approximate) order-to-delivery lead time.

## 3  An EastWest Transport Corridor (EWTC) Scenario

In a scenario around the Southern Baltic Sea we studied three types of transport measures aimed at achieving a modal shift from road to rail and sea transportation, which is an explicit goal within the European Union [4]. We studied a kilometer tax for heavy trucks in Sweden, a $CO_2$ tax for all transports in the studied area, and a new direct railway link between Karlshamn and Älmhult (the so-called SouthEast Link). Possible consequences are changes in mode and route choices, transport costs, emissions, etc. The studied kilometer tax level is suggested by the Swedish Institute for Communication Analysis (SIKA) [5] and it is differentiated based on the euro class and on the total weight of trucks. We investigated a range of $CO_2$ tax levels, which are in line with the levels discussed in another report by SIKA [18]. The SouthEast Link is an infrastructure project that is currently discussed in Sweden, and in the study we investigated two different timetables for the considered link.

The presented scenario, which is illustrated in Fig. 2, is an extension of a scenario that has been studied earlier in collaboration with partners in a project financed by the EU (http://www.eastwesttc.org). It contains one logistical terminal in Kaunas (Lithuania), which provides two types of products, and three typical customers in the studied area; one in Sweden (Älmhult) and two in Denmark (Copenhagen and Esbjerg). In the scenario, transport by rail, road, and sea is offered by five transport providers, and there are several possible routes for transporting 20 ft ISO-containers (TEUs) from Kaunas to the three customers. In the scenario, transportation by sea and rail is assumed to follow timetables while transportation by road is demand driven. A detailed description of the scenario, including input parameters for all entities, timetables, etc., is provided in [7].

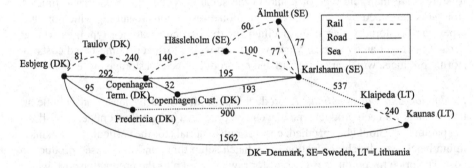

**Fig. 2.** Illustration of the transport network modeled in the studied scenario, where the numbers on the links represent distances in kilometers

The input data used in the scenario has been collected from different sources (e.g., http://www.ntm.a.se/). Since the aim was to mirror a real-world scenario, we have used data from existing companies in the studied region as much as possible. However, since the case study models future scenarios, it has not always been possible to make use of real data. Therefore, it was necessary to make certain assumptions, e.g., concerning train frequencies on the SouthEast Link, consumption, customer behavior, and average load utilization for different types of transports. The behaviors of the decision makers are restricted to how they are internally modeled, and they have to communicate with each other according to the interaction protocol in TAPAS. In particular, for the customer we made assumptions regarding order quantities, delivery time windows, safety-stock levels and inventory holding costs.

The scenario and its results have been validated through interviews with domain experts, and a visualization of the scenario helped us discover unrealistic assumptions and to facilitate the communication of assumptions and simulation results. We have performed sensitivity analyses regarding different input parameters in order to understand how different parameters influence the results. In the sensitivity analysis we mainly analyzed load utilization factors of different vehicles and storage interest rates, for improved understanding and for calibration of the scenario. As part of the study we also studied different levels of a $CO_2$ tax to analyze how different tax levels may influence the transport system. Moreover, the estimated transport cost structures, i.e., the relations between time-based and distance-based costs have been compared to the cost structures used in the SAMGODS model [19].

In the simulation study we considered the following experimental settings:

**S0.** The base case refers to the current situation without any of the studied measures.
**S1.** S0 + a kilometer tax of 0.15 euro/km for trucks operating in Sweden, and between Copenhagen Terminal and Copenhagen Customer.
**S2.** S0 + a $CO_2$ tax for all vehicles operating in the modeled region. Tax levels from 0.10 euro/kg up to 0.30 euro/kg in steps of 0.05 were considered. We let S2.$x$ refer to setting S2 with a $CO_2$ tax level of 0.$x$ euro/kg.
**S3.** S0 + a new railway link between Karlshamn and Älmhult (i.e., the SouthEast Link). Two timetables, which are synchronized in different ways with ferry arrivals in Karlshamn (from Klaipeda), were considered: a) worse synchronization and b) better synchronization (see [7] for timetables).

For each setting we simulated 420 days with a precision of 1 minute.

To be able to obtain results with statistical significance we made simulation runs with 10 sets of random generator seeds for variation of consumption (different seeds were used for different customers). Each set of seeds was used for all settings, which enabled us to make pair-wise comparisons of results for different settings.

From a larger set of available routes, we observed that only the following five routes were used, however in different proportions for different settings:

**Route 1.** Kaunas (Rail) Klaipeda (Sea) Karlshamn (Road) Älmhult
**Route 2.** Kaunas (Rail) Klaipeda (Sea) Karlshamn (Rail) Älmhult
**Route 3.** Kaunas (Rail) Klaipeda (Sea) Karlshamn (Rail) Copenhagen Terminal (Road) Copenhagen Customer
**Route 4.** Kaunas (Rail) Klaipeda (Sea) Karlshamn (Road) Copenhagen Customer
**Route 5.** Kaunas (Rail) Klaipeda (Sea) Fredericia (Road) Esbjerg

An important indicator of the impact of the studied transport measures is the route choice, which we illustrate with the percentage of TEUs transported using different routes. In Table 1 it can be seen that all of the studied measures caused a shift towards routes involving more rail transports and less road transports. However, for different measures the shift was observed in different parts of the network. For transportation to Älmhult, the only measure that showed an effect on the route choice is the South-East Link. In the settings without the SouthEast Link, all TEUs were transported on road between Karlshamn and Älmhult (i.e., Route 1). In the settings with the South-East Link (S3a and S3b) we observed shifts toward Route 2 using the SouthEast Link (i.e., railway). In S3a in average 5.8% and in S3b in average 43.6% of the TEUs were transported using Route 2. Not surprisingly, in the setting with better timetable synchronization (S3b) we observed a higher shift than in the setting with slightly worse synchronization (S3a). In all settings, transportation of all TEUs to Esbjerg were made using Route 5, with sea transportation from Klaipeda to Fredericia followed by road transportation from Fredericia to Esbjerg. This is reasonable due to the fact that the long distance makes it economically tractable to use sea transportation instead of land transportation through Sweden and Denmark. For Copenhagen Customer, which can be reached only by truck, the results vary for the different settings. For settings S0 and S3, in which no measures were applied for transportation on the routes to Copenhagen Customer, all transports were made using road transportation from Karlshamn directly to Copenhagen Customer (i.e., Route 4). In setting S1 (kilometer tax), a 100 % shift towards Route 3 using rail between Karlshamn and Copenhagen Terminal followed by road transportation between Copenhagen Terminal and Copenhagen Customer was observed. For settings S2 (CO$_2$ tax), a gradually increasing shift towards Route 3 was observed as the tax level was increased.

**Table 1.** For each setting and each customer, the average taken over 10 replications of the share of TEUs (in percentage) transported using the different routes

|  |  | S0 | S1 | S2.10 | S2.15 | S2.20 | S2.25 | S2.30 | S3a | S3b |
|---|---|---|---|---|---|---|---|---|---|---|
| Älmhult | Route 1 | 100 | 100 | 100 | 100 | 100 | 100 | 100 | 94.2 | 56.4 |
|  | Route 2 | 0 | 0 | 0 | 0 | 0 | 0 | 0 | 5.8 | 43.6 |
| Copenhagen | Route 3 | 0 | 100 | 49.6 | 49.6 | 66.0 | 78.5 | 100 | 0 | 0 |
|  | Route 4 | 100 | 0 | 50.4 | 50.4 | 34.0 | 21.5 | 0 | 100 | 100 |
| Esbjerg | Route 5 | 100 | 100 | 100 | 100 | 100 | 100 | 100 | 100 | 100 |

A positive consequence of achieving a shift from road to rail transportation is reduced CO$_2$ emissions. All observed reductions of CO$_2$ emissions in the studied system is a consequence of a modal shift from road to rail in Sweden and Denmark. Therefore, in Fig. 3 we present the relative CO$_2$ reduction for (a) the whole system, and (b) land transports in Sweden and Denmark. The main reason for observing such a minor reduction of CO$_2$ emissions when considering all simulated transports is that a significant share of the transports in all settings were made using sea and rail transportation between Kaunas and Karlshamn and between Klaipeda and Esbjerg. Further, the transport costs are affected in different ways by different measures and it may be important to analyze the positive effects (e.g., reduced CO$_2$ emissions) in relation to the economic impact caused by applying measures. For the studied transport measures, we show in Table 2 the average costs for transporting one TEU to the different customers.

For transportation to Älmhult, we observed a very small change in transport cost when studying the effects of the SouthEast Link (S3a and S3b). The reason is that the costs for transportation by road and rail between Karlshamn and Älmhult in the studied scenario are rather similar. The cost for transportation to the customer in Copenhagen is affected both by the studied CO$_2$ tax and by the kilometer tax, since it is impossible to reach the customer without involving road transportation. The cost for transportation to Esbjerg is only influenced by an increased CO$_2$ tax, since all transports to Esbjerg is made with sea and rail transportation, which is not affected by the studied kilometer tax.

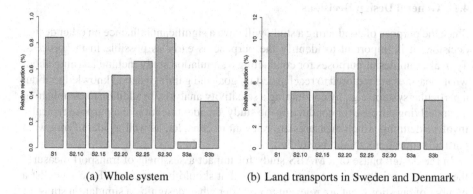

(a) Whole system        (b) Land transports in Sweden and Denmark

**Fig. 3.** For each studied measure, the relative reduction (in percentage) of $CO_2$ emissions for (a) the whole system, and (b) land transports in Sweden and Denmark

**Table 2.** For each setting, the average cost (in euro) for transporting one TEU to each customer

|            | S0    | S1    | S2.10 | S2.15 | S2.20 | S2.25 | S2.30 | S3a   | S3b   |
|------------|-------|-------|-------|-------|-------|-------|-------|-------|-------|
| Älmhult    | 364.2 | 368.5 | 426.0 | 456.9 | 487.8 | 518.7 | 549.6 | 364.7 | 364.3 |
| Copenhagen | 554.8 | 566.3 | 627.3 | 660.9 | 695.4 | 729.4 | 764.5 | 554.9 | 554.8 |
| Esbjerg    | 519.0 | 519.0 | 606.9 | 650.8 | 694.7 | 738.6 | 782.6 | 519.0 | 519.0 |

## 4 Discussion on How to Conduct MABS Studies for Impact Assessment of Transport Measures

In this section, we discuss a number of aspects that are important to consider when using MABS for impact assessment of different types of transport measures. The discussion is built around the TAPAS simulation tool described in Section 2 and the EWTC simulation study presented in Section 3, and we provide concrete examples of lessons learnt when working with TAPAS. Overviews of different aspects that are relevant to consider when conducting simulation studies can be found in the literature, e.g., design of simulation studies are discussed in [10,9,11], data collection in [16], verification and validation in [17], and output data analysis in [12].

The process of conducting a simulation study can be regarded as a process containing three sequential phases; design, execution and analysis. In the *design phase*, the analyst finds out what should be done, and decides how it is appropriate to conduct the study. In the *execution phase*, input data is collected, scenarios are coded, and simulation runs are made. Finally, in the *analysis phase*, the output is analyzed and potentially generalized to enable general conclusions to be made. The process is typically iterative since there often is a need to return to previous phases and reconsider earlier decisions and activities. For example, from a pre-study it may be realized that the ambitions concerning data collection, generalization, complexity of the studied scenario, etc., may have to be revised.

## 4.1  General Design Decisions

Since the purpose of conducting a study will have a significant influence on other design decisions it is important to identify the purpose as early as possible in the process. Typical examples of purposes for conducting a simulation study include learning about what measures are required to reach a certain goal and gaining general knowledge about a particular system, e.g., by conducting a sensitivity analysis. In addition to establishing an underlying purpose for conducting the study, the identification of a purpose typically involves defining which measures are relevant to consider, as well as identifying what particular questions should be studied.

In the design phase of a MABS study for impact assessment of transport measures there are potentially many design questions that should be answered. Below we list a number of questions that are relevant to consider when designing a simulation study, of which some are general and also discussed in the literature [9]:

- What particular set of transport measures should be studied?
- What is the expected outcome of the study, i.e., which types of effects are expected?
- What is an appropriate scope of the studied scenario considering complexity and the potential to obtain useful results (e.g., concerning which physical entities and what geographical areas should be considered)?
- Should the scenario be calibrated towards current practice, and how should it be calibrated?
- How should the scenario and the results be validated?
- If (and how) should a sensitivity analysis be conducted?
- What output data is relevant to study, and how should the output be analyzed?
- Is there a need to generalize the results, and how is it appropriate to obtain generalizable results?
- From which data sources should data be collected, and how should data be preprocessed?
- How should prices and costs be represented? Is it relevant to model estimated internal costs, or is it better to model market prices of services, which potentially include profit margins?
- Which physical entities should be represented, and how is it appropriate to model them? For example, is it relevant to aggregate entities of the same type (e.g., product types as in the studied EWTC scenario)?
- How and which decision makers should be represented in the model, e.g., concerning how decision strategies are assigned to agents?
- How many simulation runs should be made, what parameter settings should be used for the different runs, and how long should simulation runs be?

## 4.2  Input Data Management

When conducting a MABS study for impact assessment of transport measures, it is important to identify all entities that should be modeled, and describe them in an appropriate level of detail. Input data for describing physical entities, e.g., vehicle characteristics, link lengths and timetables, should be collected. In TAPAS, input distributions should be specified for consumption, production, and transportation. Also, strategies of modeled decision makers, specified as cost structures, need to be provided. In most realistic scenarios, this means that a large amount of input data need to be collected from various sources, and this is something that generally applies to micro-level simulation. There are several issues related to collecting input data, e.g., crucial (micro-level) data might be missing or difficult to obtain. Typical reasons are that data do not exist, or that organizations and enterprises that are holding information are unwilling to share detailed and accurate data. Further, the quality of available data may be low, and data collection may require too much time and effort. Therefore, the analyst sometimes needs to make a trade-off between how much effort should be spent on data collection and the possibility to obtain high quality data, and ultimately, high quality results.

If data is partially or completely inaccurate or missing, appropriate assumptions about the reality may have to be made to be able to represent those entities that are completely or partially unknown. For example, to be able to study certain transport related taxes and fees, it is sometimes necessary to break down the transport cost into cost parameters, such as time-based and distance-based costs. If the relations between these cost parameters are unknown, the analyst has to make proper assumptions and estimations. This is exactly what was done in the EWTC study, in which time-based and distance-based cost parameters were estimated and validated using interviews with domain experts and with macro-level data from the SAMGODS model [19].

Due to limited availability of data or when the need for a high level of detail in the scenario is low, it may sometimes be appropriate to aggregate multiple real-world entities into fewer entities in the model, e.g., by using available aggregated (macro-level) data. As an example, in the EWTC study producers have been aggregated and represented by a single logistical terminal, and product types are also represented on an aggregate level. On the contrary, if accurate data is available it is sometimes possible and relevant to represent a real world entity with multiple model entities, e.g., when the same type of entity is associated with different costs in different geographical areas. Moreover, depending on the purpose of a study, it is sometimes relevant to disregard input that is assumed to have little or no effect on the decision making and on the types of output that are studied. For example, if no measures or effects concerning emissions are considered, it is typically not relevant to provide input data related to emissions.

An option that is always possible when dealing with issues concerning availability of high-quality input data is to narrow the scope (e.g., geographical) of the scenario to a size for which appropriate data can be found. However, it is important to consider that the validity and possibility for generalizing the results may be affected when assuming or aggregating data, or when the scope of the study is being reduced.

A question that is related to management of input data is if internal cost structures of the modeled companies should be modeled, or if it is better to model market prices of services, potentially including profit margins. It should be noted that it often is difficult to obtain data that accurately estimate internal cost structures, e.g., since companies are unwilling to share data, or since the study concerns future scenarios for which no real-world data exists. It might be better to use market prices when they appear to be rather stable and representative for long-term prices of transport services whereas internal costs, if available, might be more suitable in other cases. Internal costs may have the advantage to better represent different cost components (e.g., time- and distance-based costs), which might be important when analyzing different transport measures, whereas market prices rarely are given explicitly for different cost components. Also, internal cost estimates might be more accurate in case of non-stable or unknown market prices, e.g., if a new market or newly introduced product types are studied.

### 4.3  Validation, Verification and Calibration

Validation, verification, and calibration of simulation models and scenarios are important in order to obtain valid and credible results [13]. Verification concerns whether an implemented simulation model represents a correct mapping of the conceptual model. Validation is about determining if the conceptual model represents a correct mapping of the modeled system. Calibration is about tuning the parameters of a simulation model or a scenario, typically in an iterative manner by comparing simulation output to real system output, in order to obtain valid simulation results. Complete validity is often difficult to obtain, and the level of validity and credibility that is needed depends on the purpose of the model [17]. A considerable amount of effort typically has to be put into setup and calibration of scenarios. It should be noted that the process of conducting simulation experiments typically contributes to the validity of the model.

From the wide range of available techniques for validation and verification (see [17] for an overview), it is the responsibility of the analyst to determine on case basis how the validity should be shown. A few examples of techniques that can be used include:

- Involving decision makers and policy makers when developing scenarios.
- Comparing results with historic and recent real-world data, with statistics concerning activities in the studied area, and with results obtained with other models.
- Conducting sensitivity analyses of certain input parameters and assess the behavior of the studied system.
- Performing pre-studies with small versions of the scenario, which would make the results easier to compare with analytically generated output and enabling results to be compared with what is to be logically expected.

Moreover, to (partially) validate a model or a scenario, it is possible to use conceptual validation, i.e., "determining that the theories and assumptions underlying the conceptual model are correct and that the model representation of the problem entity is 'reasonable' for the intended purpose of the model" [17].

We believe it is important to involve different stakeholders in the process of formulating scenarios. By making use of participatory modeling, the process of formulating a scenario will also be part of the process of understanding and analyzing the impact of transport measures. The EWTC scenario was developed in collaboration with a number of relevant stakeholders, such as, transport authorities, transport operators and regional government, from three countries. A rough sketch of the scenario, including the scope of the scenario, interesting transport measures, relevant effects and types of goods, etc., was developed during discussions in this group. Then the simulation experts developed a more detailed scenario, which was presented to the group. After a discussion the group proposed some refinements of the suggested scenario. When the simulation experiments had been run, the results were analyzed within the group.

Involving policy makers and transport companies in the design of a MABS model is also important to discuss which aspects are necessary, relevant and desirable to represent. In the case of TAPAS, the model was developed in projects with the involvement of various transport companies, transport analysts, and policy makers, and this process is still ongoing in a couple of projects even if the model already is implemented.

A typical approach when conducting a simulation study is to compare the results of a base scenario, which often is calibrated to correspond to the current situation, with the results of a number of situations in which one or more measures are applied. Parameters should (if possible) be calibrated in a way that the base scenario and the extended scenarios are affected in a similar way, however, this is something that can be difficult to achieve.

In real-world transport chains, decisions that are ineffective from a cost perspective are sometimes taken, e.g., due to old habit or since costs are estimated incorrectly by decision makers. If a purpose is to mimic a current (potentially non-optimal) situation, it is possible to compensate for non-optimal behavior by calibrating certain input parameters (costs, load utilization factors, etc.). A further possibility is to explicitly model non-optimal behavior of real-world decision makers, e.g., by modeling that it may take some time before a change of transport solution occurs, even though there exists other more beneficial solutions. It would also be possible to let factors such as environmental impact, reliability and punctuality, explicitly influence the decision making. Another reason for calibrating a scenario (other than representing non-optimal behavior) is to compensate for errors in input data.

## 4.4 Result Analysis and Generalization

In TAPAS, all input data and activities that occur during a simulation run are logged in a database, which makes it possible to reproduce and carefully analyze simulation runs afterwards. We argue that it could be a good idea to keep a database containing all relevant information concerning a simulation run, in contrast to just saving specific types of output, unless this is considered infeasible from a performance perspective. This is due to the fact that it could be realized late in a study what particular output data is needed. However, for large scenarios that create huge amount of output data, it is often impractical, or even impossible, to store all data that is produced during a simulation run. Examples of relevant output data that can be extracted from TAPAS are choices of vehicle types and transport routes, order sizes and frequencies, transport times, transport costs, environmental performance (e.g., $CO_2$ emissions), and transport work (ton kilometers).

The output from TAPAS can be categorized into economical, logistical, and environmental, which makes it possible to use TAPAS for multi-criteria analysis. In the EWTC scenario, $CO_2$ emissions, costs, and modal split were analyzed, enabling the analyst and policy makers to use multiple aspects when analyzing the results of a transport measure, or when assessing if the expected impact of a transport measure is sufficiently sustainable. An advantage of making use of MABS for transport policy analysis is that the results become rather concrete and straight-forward to relate to actual effects.

Since simulation often is considered to be a statistical experiment (activities occur according to stochastic input distributions), the output will also be randomly distributed. In TAPAS, consumption, transportation and production is described using random distributions, and to be able to draw strong conclusions, it is important to manage statistics in a proper way, e.g., by choosing input distributions carefully and analyzing output statistically. Output data can be analyzed using significance tests, correlation analyses, and by generating confidence intervals (e.g., [12]). Also, to obtain statistical significance, a larger number of replications typically need to be run for each studied setting.

Depending on what types of questions are studied, there is sometimes a wish to generalize the results. Due to difficulties regarding performance of micro-level simulation and collection of real-world data, it may be appropriate to study limited transport networks when using MABS models. However, generalizable results can still be obtained by studying a larger number of smaller scenarios in which, e.g., the location and characteristics of customers and producers are randomly varied. By simulating a range of different actors and settings, it is typically possible to observe more general tendencies than can be obtained by only simulating smaller networks.

## 5   Concluding Remarks

We have provided a discussion on how it is appropriate to design and conduct simulation studies when using MABS for impact assessment of transport policy and infrastructure measures (transport measures). The discussion concerns general design issues, input data management, validation and verification, calibration, output data analysis, and generalization of results. Specific aspects that are covered in the discussion are participatory and collaborative modeling and simulation, selection of which entities and aspects to include in a simulation study, and how multi-criteria analysis can be used with MABS when analyzing transport measures. Further, the discussion is built around the TAPAS simulation tool (see Section 2) and an EWTC simulation study (see Section 3), which illustrates how it is possible to analyze transport measures by studying modal split, $CO_2$ emissions, and transport costs.

We conclude the paper by stating that we believe that our work may be a valuable resource when (1) developing new MABS models for impact assessment of transport measures, since it is important already at the development phase to account for how to use the model, and (2) conducting simulation studies using existing models, since our discussion covers most aspects that are relevant to consider when conducting a study for impact assessment of transport measures.

**Acknowledgements.** We wish to thank our colleagues in the EWTC I and II projects for valuable feedback. The research is part-financed by the European Union (European Regional Development Fund and European Neighbourhood and Partnership Instrument, Baltic Sea Region Programme 2007-2013) via the EWTC II project.

# References

1. Button, K.: Transport Economics, 2nd edn. Edward Elgar Publishing Limited, Glos (1997)
2. Davidsson, P., Holmgren, J., Persson, J.A., Ramstedt, L.: Multi agent based simulation of transport chains. In: Proceedings of the 7th International Joint Conference on Autonomous Agents and Multiagent Systems (AAMAS 2008), May 12-16, pp. 1153–1160. International Foundation for Autonomous Agents and Multiagent Systems, Estoril (2008)
3. de Jong, G., Ben-Akiva, M.: A micro-simulation model of shipment size and transport chain choice. Transportation Research Part B 41(9), 950–965 (2007)
4. European Commission: White paper - European transport policy for 2010: time to decide. Tech. rep., Luxemburg (2001)
5. Friberg, G., Flack, M., Hill, P., Johansson, M., Vierth, I., McDaniel, J., Lundgren, T., Hesselborn, P., Bångman, G.: Kilometerskatt för lastbilar - Effekter på näringar och regioner. Redovisning av ett regeringsuppdrag i samverkan med ITPS. Report 2007:2, Swedish Institute for Transport and Communications Analysis, SIKA (2007)
6. Gambardella, L., Rizzoli, A., Funk, P.: Agent-based planning and simulation of combined rail/road transport. Simulation 78(5), 293–303 (2002)
7. Holmgren, J.: An extended EastWest Transport Corridor (EWTC) scenario (2011), http://www.bth.se/tek/jhm.nsf/attachments/eewtc_pdf/$file/eewtc.pdf
8. Holmgren, J., Davidsson, P., Persson, J.A., Ramstedt, L.: TAPAS: A multi-agent-based model for simulation of transport chains. Simulation Modelling Practice and Theory 23, 1–18 (2012)
9. Kelton, W.D., Barton, R.R.: Experimental design for simulation. In: Proceedings of the 2003 Winter Simulation Conference, December 7-10, pp. 59–65. IEEE, New Orleans (2003)
10. Kleijnen, J.P.C.: An overview of the design and analysis of simulation experiments for sensitivity analysis. European Journal of Operational Research 164(2), 287–300 (2005)
11. Kleijnen, J.P.C.: Design of experiments: overview. In: Proceedings of the 2008 Winter Simulation Conference, December 7-10, pp. 479–488. IEEE, Miami (2008)
12. Law, A.M.: Statistical analysis of simulation output data: the practical state of the art. In: Proceedings of the 2007 Winter Simulation Conference, December 9-12, pp. 77–83. IEEE, Washington, DC (2007)
13. Law, A.M., Kelton, W.D.: Simulation modelling and analysis, 3rd edn. McGraw-Hill, Singapore (2000)
14. Liedtke, G.: Principles of micro-behavior commodity transport modeling. Transportation Research Part E 45(5), 795–809 (2009)
15. Rich, J., Bröcker, J., Hansen, C.O., Korchenewych, A., Nielsen, O.A., Vuk, G.: Report on scenario, traffic forecast and analysis of traffic on the TEN-T, taking into consideration the external dimension of the union - TRANS-TOOLS version 2; Model and data improvements. Tech. rep., Copenhagen, Denmark (2009)
16. Sapsford, R., Jupp, V. (eds.): Data collection and analysis, 2nd edn. SAGE Publications Ltd., Chennai (2006)
17. Sargent, R.G.: Verification and validation of simulation models. In: Proceedings of the 2005 Winter Simulation Conference, December 4-7, pp. 130–143. IEEE, Orlando (2005)
18. SIKA: Vilken koldioxidskatt krävs för att nå framtida utsläppsmål? PM 2008:4, Swedish Institute for Transport and Communications Analysis, SIKA (2008)
19. Swahn, H.: The Swedish national model systems for goods transport SAMGODS - a brief introductory overview. SAMPLAN Report 2001:1, Swedish Institute for Transport and Communications Analysis, SIKA (2001)
20. Tavasszy, L., Smeenk, B., Ruijgrok, C.: A DSS for modelling logistic chains in freight transport policy analysis. International Transactions in Operational Research 5(6), 447–459 (1998)

# An Agent-Based Simulation of Employing Social Norms in Energy Conservation in Households

Bastin Tony Roy Savarimuthu[1], Maryam Purvis[1], and Harko Verhagen[2]

[1] University of Otago, Dunedin, P O Box 56, Dunedin, New Zealand
[2] Department of Computer and System Sciences, Stockholm University, Sweden
{tonyr,tehrany}@infoscience.otago.ac.nz, verhagen@dsv.su.se

**Abstract.** Social norms play an important role in shaping human behaviour. They guide people how to behave under certain circumstances by informing what is permitted and prohibited. Research works have shown that social norms can be successfully employed in promoting sustainable practices such as energy conservation. In particular, the combined effect of descriptive and injunctive norms has been shown to bear a positive influence in shaping social behaviour and is being employed by organizations for social norm marketing. Towards the goal of facilitating the reduction of energy consumption in households, this simulation-based study investigates three simple agent-based models (global, local and similarity models) for spreading social norms based behaviour. In this context, first, the effectiveness of adopting a descriptive norm is compared across the three different models. Second, the role of combining both descriptive and injunctive norms on the reduction of energy utilization is investigated. Third, a meta-norm based intervention approach is proposed and investigated which aims at increasing the rate at which a society can converge to a decreased value of energy consumption in a society.

## 1 Introduction

Social norms are *generalized expectations of behaviour* in a society [9]. When a social norm is in-force, members of a society expect other members of the society to behave in a certain way in a given situation. Norms have been employed by human societies to facilitate cooperation and coordination among agents which enable smoother functioning of the society. Social norms are increasingly being employed in the domain called social norms approach (or social norms marketing) [18], where social norms are used to influence (or nudge) people into pursuing appropriate social behaviour. Examples of such approaches include social norm based campaigns to reduce alcohol consumption among university students [6], reduction in energy consumption in households [18], and increasing recycling [17]. In many of these social domains the actual social norm might not be known to the individuals. However, social-norm marketers are able to infer the social norm at the aggregate level through surveys. The norms thus identified can be used for providing social nudges towards facilitating behaviour modification.

Inspired by the works on social-norms based approach to social problems, this work investigates three different models that can be employed in the reduction of energy consumption in households through simulations. This paper is organized as follows.

S. Cranefield and I. Song (Eds.): PRIMA 2011 Workshops, LNAI 7580, pp. 16–31, 2012.

Section 2 discusses the related work. Section 3 presents the three models and compares the amount of energy saving obtained when certain percentage of agents of the society adopt the *energy conservation norm*. Section 4 investigates the effect of employing *injunctive norms* along with descriptive norms in the energy consumption in an agent society. Additionally, Section 5 proposes and discusses a norm-based intervention approach after certain norm emergence threshold is reached in a society to bring about faster convergence towards a reduced energy usage in the society. The limitations of the current work and the pointers towards future is provided in Section 6. Conclusions are provided in Section 7.

## 2    Background

Social norms, in particular, the combination of descriptive and injunctive norms have been shown to encourage pro-environmental behaviour such as reduction in the amount of energy used by households [18]. According to Kitts and Chiang [11] the definitions of descriptive and injunctive norms are as follows. *Descriptive norms are typical patterns of behavior, generally accompanied by the expectation that people will behave according to the pattern. Injunctive norms are prescriptive (or proscriptive) rules specifying behavior that persons ought (or ought not) to engage in.* According to Reno et al. [14], a descriptive norm defines what is commonly done in a particular circumstance and a injunctive norm defines what an agent should or shouldn't do in a particular circumstance (or what is approved or disapproved by others in a particular circumstance)[1]. Note that the definitions provided by Kitts and Chiang [11] and Reno et al. [14] are in agreement.

A general description of a social norm as given by Elster [7] is as follows: *"For norms to be social, they must be shared by other people and partly sustained by their approval and disapproval. ..."*. Thus, the definitions of descriptive and injunctive norms together capture the essence of what social norms are.

We note that a descriptive norm can be viewed as a convention (i.e. what is normally observed) and the injunctive norm elevates the status of the convention to a proper social norm through prescriptions and proscriptions. For example, assume that left-hand driving is a convention in the society. When it is a convention, the left-hand action is what people normally do in that particular society. However, this convention can become a social norm if it is prescribed (i.e. any deviations from this norm are sanctioned).

### 2.1    Related Work

This sub-section provides an overview of the related work in the area of social norm based approaches that have been employed in different domains to encourage behaviour modification, with a particular focus on the energy domain.

Researchers have found that social norm based messages help in bringing about positive changes in domains such as littering in public places [4], alcohol consumption [6], resource stealing (petrified wood stealing in Arizona national park [3]), reuse

---

[1] We note that disapproval and approval can be viewed as sanction and encouragement respectively.

(e.g. reusing hotel towels [8]) and energy conservation [18]. In particular, these works note that both descriptive and injunctive norms should be used in conjunction for facilitating a positive behavioural change. Descriptive norm on their own do not encourage positive behaviour to a large extent and in some cases boomerang effects were observed [15, 18] resulting in mixed benefits in the usage of social norms. For example, when the messages based on descriptive norm informing users that they consume low energy than their neighbours was sent, *boomerang effect* was observed where the users started consuming higher amount of energy [18] than their previous consumption. The boomerang effect was eliminated when the injunctive norms were added.

In the work of Schultz et al. [18] the objective was to examine the influence of descriptive and injunctive norms on overall reduction in energy consumption in households using a social norm based approach. The messages constructed using social norms approach is based on the average energy consumed in the neighbourhood of 290 houses. The energy consumption of all the houses in the neighbourhood is used to compute the minimum, maximum and average energy in the neighbourhood and these values are used to construct the normative messages. The descriptive norm based messages contained information about an individual household's energy usage and whether its energy consumption was below or above the average energy consumption of the neighbourhood. Households that consumed energy higher than the average tended to decrease their energy consumption. On the other hand, households that consumed less energy than the average increased their energy consumption (i.e. the boomerang effect). The authors have demonstrated that combining injunctive norms with descriptive norms eliminated the boomerang effect. A limitation of the work of Schultz et al. [18] is that they have not considered the different attributes of households that impact their energy consumption. A neighbourhood may contain households that vary in different dimensions. For example, the attributes that may impact energy usage may include: number of individuals living at home, size of homes, different appliances used, lifestyle choices (e.g. using dryer vs. hanging clothes outside) etc. These are not explicitly considered by this model. It treats the entire neighbourhood as one unit without considering the differences in energy usages driven by varying parameters. These parameters can be used to group different households into different groups and can then be used to compare the deviations in energy consumptions between members belonging to the same group.

The social norms approach used by OPOWER [1] makes use of a similarity-based approach to encourage people to reduce their energy consumption. The company sent out letters to 600,000 consumers in the United States indicating the household's energy consumption, the household average energy consumption of similar neighbours, and the energy consumption of the efficient neighbours. The document sent is the descriptive norm based nudge from OPOWER to encourage households to reduce energy consumption. The document also contained an injunctive norm based message. A smiley-based approach was used to indicate approvals for energy usage below average and disapproval for usage above average. For example, to indicate the approval one smiley was used if the energy consumption of a household was lower than average (also described in words as good) and two smileys were used to indicate that the household's average energy consumption was considerably lower than average (less than 20th percentile of energy also described in words as "great"). According to Allcott [10] this leads to 1.1%

to 2.8% reduction in the amount of energy consumption with reference to a baseline model which does not employ norms.

While Schultz et al. [18] employ a neighbourhood model, the approach used by OPOWER as discussed by Allcott [10] makes use of a similarity model. In this work, first, we investigate three types of models for norm-based influence on users behaviour using an agent-based simulation approach. The three models we investigate are the global model, local model and similarity model. These models are discussed and compared in the next section.

## 3   Investigations of Three Models for Norm-Based Social Influence

The three models investigated for norm-based social influence are the global model, local model and the similarity model. These three models were investigated in the context of the adoption of a descriptive norm in a society of agents using an agent-based social simulation (ABSS) approach [5][2].

### 3.1   Global Model

In the global model, a society of agents is simulated. Agents represent individual houses. Each agent has certain parameters. The parameters are a) a unique identifier of the house, b) the number of people living in the house and c) the energy consumed per month in Kilowatt hour (KWh) by the household. We used the data available from the Government of South Australia[3] for initializing the average energy consumption of agents. We modelled households with members ranging from one to five. The average energy consumed by the households per month is given in Table 1.

Table 1. Average energy consumption in households based on number of occupants (data from the Government of South Australia)

| Number of people in the house | Average energy consumed per month (KWh) |
|---|---|
| 1 | 479 |
| 2 | 642 |
| 3 | 738 |
| 4 | 829 |
| 5 | 1188 |

In this model, agents were randomly initialized with the number of people living in a household. Since our model considers households with sizes ranging from one to five, 20% of agents have the same value for the number of members in the household. The energy consumed by a household was initialized with a value that lies within plus or minus $x$% of the average energy consumed by household. For example, if $x$ is set to 25,

---

[2] For a general overview of the mechanisms used by researchers in the simulation-based studies of norms refer to the work of Savarimuthu and Cranefield [16].

[3] http://tinyurl.com/3fhssbf

an agent representing a household with five members will be initialized with a value that lies between 891 and 1485.

After initialization, we assume that normative messages are sent to each agent (either electronically or by post) which informs the agents about the average energy consumption of the entire society and whether their energy consumption is above or below the average. Note that the message is the descriptive norm that is being conveyed to the agents. In this model we assume that $y\%$ of agents that consume more energy than average choose to decrease their energy by $z\%$. For example if y=5 and z=5, that implies that 5% of the agents that consume more than average energy reduce their energy consumption by 5%. We also have set a buffer range, $\pm\alpha$, around the current average energy consumed in the society which governs the limit upon reaching which the agents do not have to reduce their energy any further. This buffer range has been set in order to prevent agents from perpetually decreasing their energy until they reach a value of zero and doing so will not be realistic.

In order to understand these variables better let us consider the following example. Assume that agent A has five members and its current energy consumption for the month is 1680 KWh. Assume that the agent wants to reduce its energy consumption since its consumption is higher than the 1180 KWh which is the average energy consumption as informed to the agent through the normative message. So, the agent decreases its consumption value to 1410.75 KWh (assuming z=5). Assuming the buffer value of $\alpha$=5, in further iterations if the agent decides to decrease it energy usage, it can do so to a minimum of 1247.4 assuming that average energy consumption in the society does not change in the subsequent iterations. The buffer range of the society in this case is from 1128.6 to 1247.4. Note that the buffer is a sliding buffer and the minimum and maximum values depend upon the current energy consumption average of the entire population.

Each iteration of the simulation corresponds to one month in real-time. After each iteration we record the overall energy consumed in the society. This data is used to plot the average energy consumed by the society in KWh over several months.

### 3.2  Local Model

In the global model, the whole society is treated as one unit. However, in the local model, agents in a society form several neighbourhoods. In order to simulate the neighbourhood model, the agents are arranged in a two-dimensional toroidal grid. Each agent has eight neighbours. The norm-based message sent to the agent takes into account the average energy consumption of all the eight neighbours around it. In this model, unlike the global model there isn't a unique average energy consumption value that all the agents can use to compare their energy consumption values. Depending upon the neighbours, each agent will have a different value for the average energy consumed in the neighbourhood. Hence, the buffer values for each agent will be different since the neighbourhood is different for each agent. Apart from this change, all the other aspects are the same as the global model.

## 3.3   Similarity Model

In the similarity model, agents' norm-based messages report the average energy consumed by the agents that are similar to them. In our model the similarity is based on the number of members in the household. Since there are five groups, average energy consumption is calculated for all these five groups. Agents are informed about the average energy corresponding to the groups they are in. The buffer values of agents across the five groups will be different (i.e. there will be five different buffer values, one for each group). Apart from this change, all the other aspects are the same as the global model.

## 3.4   Comparison of the Three Models

One of the objectives of this work is to investigate the differences between the three models. We believe the three models represent different choices available that can be used under different circumstances. For example, a power company that knows the data about all its consumers, may choose to employ the global model for spreading normative messages. To cater for the differences in neighbourhoods (e.g. changing climatic conditions[4]), the firm may choose to employ the local model. Additionally, the firm can also choose a similarity model, by clustering households into groups based on certain properties.

Note that the work of Schultz et al. [18] has considered a neighbourhood model[5]. OPOWER has employed a similarity model. In this work, we are interested in comparing the three models by keeping the parameters constant across the models. Towards that goal, the questions we investigate are two-fold.

1. How much decrease in energy is possible using each of the models?
2. What is the rate of convergence towards reduced consumption of energy in each of these models?

In order to answer these questions we simulated an agent society with 1000 agents. The parameters that were used in the three models are given in Table 2.

The simulation set-up considers two variations in the nature of the agents that are influenced by norms (i.e. agents that consume high energy that would like to decrease energy consumption). In the first set-up, a fixed percentage of agents are assumed to be influenced by norms in the entire simulation. We call this set-up a static set-up. In the dynamic set-up, a fixed percentage of randomly chosen agents are influenced by norms in each iteration. For example, if the percentage is set to five, then the 50 agents in the society that are under the influence of norm in one iteration will be different from the agents under influence in the next iteration. This represents a society where agents that are influenced by norms are dynamic. However, in the static set-up the same 50 agents are influenced by norms throughout the entire simulation.

---

[4] Neighbourhoods differing in the number of sunshine hours may impact energy consumption.
[5] Strictly speaking, the model considered is a global model since only one neighbourhood is considered.

**Table 2.** Simulation parameters

| Parameters | Values |
|---|---|
| Number of agents | 1000 |
| Range of initialization values ($x$) | $\pm 25\%$ |
| Percentage of agents influenced by norms[6] ($y$) | 5% |
| Nature of agents influenced by norms | Static or Dynamic |
| Percentage energy decrement ($z$) | 5% |
| Buffer range around average ($\alpha$) | $\pm 5\%$ |
| Number of iterations | 1000 |
| Number of runs | 1000 |

## 3.5   Static Set-Up

We ran the simulation for each of the models under static set-up for 1000 iterations by keeping all the parameters constant across all the three models. The important details of one particular run for all the three models (keeping the random seed constant) are given in Table 3.

**Table 3.** Static set-up: comparison of three models based on one run of the simulation

| Model | Standard deviation (start) | Convergence points (months) | Percentage decrease in energy (end) |
|---|---|---|---|
| Global model | 260.16 | 15 | 2.03 |
| Local model | 245.01 | 15 | 1.88 |
| Similarity model | 112.97 | 5 | 0.81 |

Column two of Table 3 shows the standard deviation in the initialization values of agents across models. Column three shows the iteration in which convergence to a particular value of energy consumption was achieved in the model. We consider a result to have converged if the difference in the average energy consumption of the society between two consecutive iterations is less than 0.01. Column four shows the amount of decrease in energy at the end of the simulation.

Two observations can be made from the results presented in Table 3. First, it can be observed that the percentage of energy decrease in the global model is the highest and the percentage of energy decrease in the similarity model is the lowest. Second, it can be observed that agents using the similarity model converge the fastest among the three models (i.e. five months for convergence in the similarity model vs. 15 months in the other two models). Results shown in columns three and four of Table 3 can be explained using the data given in column two. It can be observed that the standard deviation for the global model is the highest. Standard deviation represents the variation in energy levels across all the agents in the society. Hence, the agents with high energy utilization in the global model contribute to the substantial lowering of energy by gradually moving towards consuming less energy (i.e. the amount of decrease to a reduced value is high).

The standard deviation for the local model is lower than the global model. So, the energy reduction using this model is lower than the global model. The standard deviation of the similarity based model is considerably lower than the other two models which implies that the agents in the model do not have larger variability in terms of energy utilization when compared to the local and global model which results in reduced lowering of energy consumption values in the end. We believe it is intuitive that similarity model will have the lowest value in standard deviation when compared to the other two models since the agents in this model have 'similar' energy consumption values (since they are grouped based on similarity).

We also conducted experiments by varying the percentage of static agents from 5% to 100% as shown in Figure 1. 1000 runs were conducted for each of the experiments. The energy consumption values obtained for these three models are given as three lines. The observations made from the results obtained for a single run of the experiment also hold for this experiment. Additionally, a third observation can be made from the result shown in Figure 1. The difference between the overall decrease in energy between the global and local models is insignificant. This is because over large number of runs, the difference between the global and local models tend to smooth out.

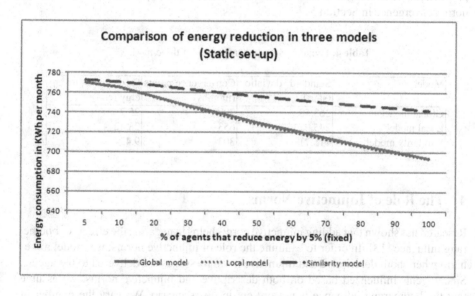

**Fig. 1.** Static set-up: A comparison of three models

## 3.6  Dynamic Set-Up

We also conducted experiments by keeping the percentage of agents that are influenced by norm fixed to 5% but allowing these 5% to be made of randomly chosen agents from an agent society[7]. This models the effect that different agents can be influenced by the norms at different points of time by choosing to decrease their energy consumption.

By keeping all the other parameters constant, we compared one run of each of the models. Figure 2 shows three lines that correspond to the the energy consumption of the society with different models. The results of this experiment are in agreement with the results of the static set-up. The difference between the results for the global and local model are due to the differences in the standard deviation between agents in the start of the experiment (see Table 4). Two additional observations can be made by comparing Table 4 with Table 3. First, the time taken to reach convergence (i.e. convergence points in months given in Column three of the tables) is longer in the dynamic set-up than the static set-up. This is expected, since the agents that are influenced dynamically change in each iteration. Second, the energy reduction of the societies are higher in the dynamic set-up than the static set-up. Even though the energy reduction is much higher in the dynamic set-up, the amount of time taken for the reduction is high (303 months which is about 25 years for the similarity model). Waiting 25 years for a norm to converge may not be quite reasonable particularly considering faster preventive measures that we would like to undertake in order to avoid greenhouse gas emissions from energy production. We investigate a meta-norm based intervention approach to facilitate faster norm convergence in Section 5.

**Table 4.** Dynamic set-up: comparison of three models

| Model | Standard deviation (start) | Convergence points (months) | % decrease in energy (end) |
|---|---|---|---|
| Global model | 263.50 | 709 | 25.7 |
| Local model | 245.01 | 653 | 23.42 |
| Similarity model | 115.71 | 303 | 9.42 |

## 4   The Role of Injunctive Norms

Research has shown that adding injunctive norms helps in negating the effects of boomerang influence [18]. In order to examine the role of injunctive norms, we model a scenario where both descriptive and injunctive norm messages are delivered to the agents. Since agents influenced based on both descriptive and injunctive norms, we assume that the boomerang influence is not present in this scenario. We vary the number of agents that are influenced by both the norms (i.e. combined influence (CI)) by 2%, 5%, 10% and 20%. All the other parameters were the same as the previous experiment

---

[7] The motivations of this set-up include the following. a) Situations of agents may change over time. An agent may not be able to conserve energy all the time. For example buying a new electric appliance or the arrival of a new-born that requires heating in an additional room may result in a more than average energy bill for the subsequent month. Hence, the change in composition of agents that reduce energy may be inevitable and that needs to be considered while modeling. b) New agents may be influenced by others and they may start conserving energy. These agents may compensate for agents that drop out.

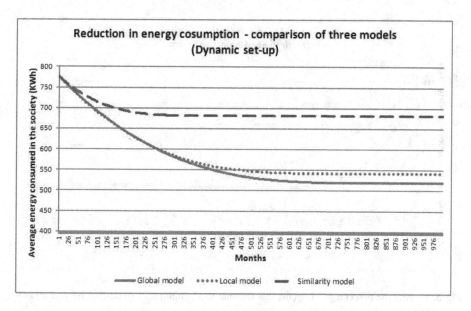

**Fig. 2.** Dynamic set-up: A comparison of three models

(see Table 2). Our objective in this experiment is to investigate what the implications are by varying the percentage of agents influenced by a combination of injunctive and descriptive norms.

It can be observed from Figure 3 that as the percentage of agents that are influenced by the norms increase, the rate of convergence is faster. The convergence points (in months) are given in Table 5. It should be noted that the values to which they converge are not significantly different. We believe modelling high acceptance rates such as 10% and 20% are reasonable because with the advent of mobile phones and social networks people can be informed and encouraged towards adopting pro-environmental behaviours instead of just using a traditional paper-based approach for spreading normative message. For example, a social-network based application for sharing energy consumption values may induce reduction in energy consumption [12] especially when members are appreciated for taking initiatives to lower carbon foot-print. Mobile phones can be used to spread normative messages instantly (e.g. SMS and Twitter messages). Additionally, a considerable proportion of phones nowadays have the ability to connect to the Internet and can access social networks with ease. Hence, they are a promising tool for spreading norm-based behaviour change. It should be noted that the convergence points achieved through higher percentages of agents changing their behaviour, (e.g., 96 months for 20% of agents reducing their energy consumption), provide some indication that reduction in energy consumption may be achieved in a reasonable time period in the future without requiring external interventions. However, for smaller percentage of agents, the convergence times are longer.

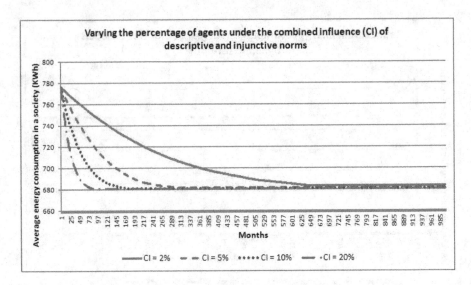

**Fig. 3.** Varying the percentage of agents that respond to a combination of descriptive and injunctive norms

**Table 5.** Convergence points on varying the percentage of agents that are influence by a combination of descriptive and injunctive norms

| % of agents | Convergence points(months) |
|:---:|:---:|
| 2 | 364 |
| 5 | 303 |
| 10 | 187 |
| 20 | 96 |

## 5   Interventions Using a Meta-norm

In this section we present how interventions can be designed based on convergence levels of agents in a society, in order to facilitate faster convergence. These interventions are based on meta-norms. Meta-norms are norms that govern norms. In our case, the meta-norm is based on the convergence value of the average energy consumption in the society.

Let us assume that 75% population of the society consume energy lower than the maximum buffer value allowed around the average energy consumption of a society. The value of 75% is the meta-norm which serves as a starting point for norm interventions at the societal level. The meta-norm is the value agreed upon by the society, where the outlier agents (i.e. agents consuming more energy) are expected to pay higher rates for energy than those who are lower than the range. For example, heavy users of energy may have to pay, say 1.1 times the normal energy price and those who consume energy less than the maximum buffer value may pay 0.9 times the normal energy price. The motivation of this meta-norm based intervention is that similar neighbours should have similar energy needs, hence incentives and disincentives should be used for encouraging and discouraging behaviours. Note that the top-down intervention is built on top of the convergence that emerges in the society using a bottom-up approach.

Note that the intervention is possible only when the society has an agreement on the value for the convergence (e.g. 75% vs. 90%), which is the meta-norm that can be derived based on a bottom-up approach such as voting. Additionally, the society should be motivated in implementing the scheme that rewards lower power consumption and penalizes high power consumption. In this work, we assume that these two conditions hold in a society. Through experimental results we show the effect of interventions, which are facilitated in the society, after certain convergence levels are achieved.

### 5.1 Effect of Meta-norm Based Interventions at Different Levels of Convergences

We investigated the effect of interventions after different levels of convergences are reached by keeping all the parameters constant. We also assumed that a certain percentage of agents will change their mind after the meta-norm intervention. As a sample value, we chose 10%. This value has been chosen to show that twice the amount of agents change their mind than the original model discussed in Section 3. Our justification for doubling the number of agents is based on the fact that humans are utility driven (most of the times) and they respond to monetary-based incentives than non-monetary based incentives as observed in other domains [2].

Figure 4 shows four lines that represent energy consumptions in societies under different intervention criteria (IC). The solid line shows the energy consumption of the society without norm interventions. The other three lines show the energy consumption of the same society before and after norm intervention. The interventions were applied for the same society under three conditions. The interventions were applied after 60%, 70% and 80% of the agents had converged to an energy consumption value below the maximum buffer value. The interventions corresponding to the three conditions were investigated in three different experiments.

It can be observed from Figure 4 that when the intervention starts earlier, the decrease in the energy consumption of the society also starts earlier (see the line corresponding to IC=60%). This results in faster norm convergence. Table 6 shows the iteration in which norm intervention was introduced (i.e. the iteration in which the society converged to a particular convergence value) and the iteration in which the society converged to a reduced energy consumption value (i.e. the difference in decrease in energy between two consecutive iterations for the entire society is less than 0.01).

### 5.2 Effect of Modifying the Percentage of Agents Influenced

For two different values of intervention criteria (65% and 75%), we varied the percentage of agents influenced (IA) by the intervention by 10%, 20% and 50%[8]. It can

---

[8] We believe utilitarian agents will start reducing their energy consumption once a price-based incentive measure has been introduced in the system through the meta-norms. The three different percentages reflect the what-if scenarios that we consider in our simulations.

**Table 6.** Intervention points and convergence points at different levels of convergence

| % Intervention Criterion (IC) | Intervention points (months) | Convergence points (months) |
|---|---|---|
| Without IC | - | 302 |
| With IC=60% | 3 | 179 |
| With IC=70% | 44 | 197 |
| With IC=80% | 112 | 227 |

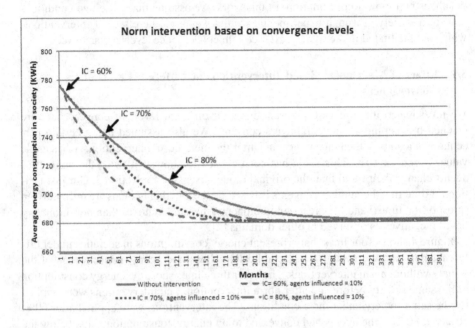

**Fig. 4.** Norm intervention based on convergence levels

be observed from Figure 5 that when the percentage of agents that are influenced increases, the convergence to a decreased energy consumption value is fast. Table 7 shows the three convergence points for different percentages of agents influenced for both the intervention criteria. It can also be observed from Figure 5 that the iterations in which the intervention comes into effect is the same for all the four cases of each of the convergence criteria (shown using arrows inside the Figure 5). However, the convergence points reached depends on the percentage of agents being influenced. Greater the percentages of agents influenced, the faster is the convergence. This graph thus shows how a meta-norm based intervention can bring about faster convergence towards reduced energy consumption in an agent society. Faster convergence towards a reduced consumption will result in cost reduction in the society. This is because the extra energy does not have to be produced. This also may have other indirect effects on the environment such as decreased $CO_2$ emissions.

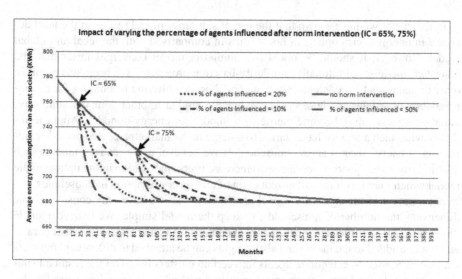

**Fig. 5.** Impact of varying the percentage of agents influenced after norm intervention

**Table 7.** Convergence points on varying the percentage of agents that are influenced after intervention

| | Convergence points | | |
|---|---|---|---|
| Intervention Criterion (IC) | IA=10% | IA=20% | IA=50% |
| 65% | 184 | 113 | 66 |
| 75% | 217 | 168 | 123 |

We believe the results shown in Figures 4 and 5 are intuitive and bear real world implications. We note that, as a society we can create meta-norms using a bottom-up approach. The employment of meta-norms and the associated price-based incentive mechanism in addition to the use of descriptive and injunctive norms may better motivate the users towards faster lowering of their energy consumption. Additionally, energy firms and the decision making bodies can use meta-norm based approach to increase the adoption rate of pro-environmental practices such as energy reduction.

## 6 Discussion

Some works on policy design for institutions have investigated the role of bottom-up (emergent or endogenous) [19] and top-down (prescriptive or exogenous) [20] approaches that facilitate behaviour modification in agent societies. They have shown that the results of policies that arise from an endogenous approach are different from those obtained from the exogenous approach. In this paper we have employed a combination of both these approaches in the context of meta-norm based intervention as discussed in Section 5.

In this paper we have shown that the use of similarity model results in the least decrease in energy consumption in households in comparison with the local and global model. However, it should be noted that similarity model converges faster than the other two models. Additionally, similarity-based approaches have been successful in other domains such as content-based and collaborative filtering techniques for recommendation of articles and books [13]. We believe, similar to other domains, similarity-based approaches may become the de-facto model for energy-domains. Applications that provide such a service have started to emerge in the marketplace that provide comparison of energy usages across households[9]. We believe, using realistic models such as similarity-based approaches may also increase users' motivation in the uptake of the model which may result in further reduction of energy consumption in households.

A limitation of the similarity model presented is that we have only considered one dimension, the number of households, to keep the model simple. We believe a single dimension should suffice for the purposes of demonstrating the approach. Other parameters can be added to the model and also weights can be attached to different parameters which can be used to categorize agents into certain clusters based on the resultant similarity scores. In the future, norm emergence on top of relevant spatial-network topologies can also be investigated. The cost of energy has not been explicitly considered in this work. However, the cost can be calculating by obtaining the product of unit price and the energy consumed.

We believe the next step is to create a social network based set-up in order to study the influence of social networks on normative behaviour. This will involve creating social network applications that would a) provide the ability for individual users to link their own energy consumption data and b) provide normative feedback using similarity-based approach and c) make use of social-network based influence to encourage reduction in energy consumption. The main challenge may lie in the integration of data from independent providers. In cases where the provider does not provide appropriate APIs to access the data, individual users may enter their energy consumption data to the social-network application. However, the trustworthiness of the data posted by users is likely to pose problems.

## 7   Conclusion

This work aimed at investigating the influence of social norms in facilitating reduced energy consumption in societies using agent-based simulations. First, three models for spreading norm-based influence were investigated namely global, local and neighbourhood models. These three models were compared in the context of spreading the descriptive norm in the society. Second, the impact of the combined effect of injunctive and descriptive norms was investigated. Third, a meta-norm based intervention approach was investigated in order to demonstrate how these interventions can result in faster reduction of energy consumption among households.

**Acknowledgments.**   The authors would like to thank Sharmila Savarimuthu and the three anonymous reviewers for their comments.

---

[9] http://www.energyaverage.co.uk/

# References

1. Opower, http://opower.com/ (last accessed, August 10, 2011)
2. Church, A.H.: Estimating the effect of incentives on mail survey response rates: A meta-analysis. Public Opinion Quarterly 57(1), 62 (1993)
3. Cialdini, R.B., Demaine, L.J., Sagarin, B.J., Barrett, D.W., Rhoads, K., Winter, P.L.: Managing social norms for persuasive impact. Social Influence 1(1), 3 (2006)
4. Cialdini, R.B., Reno, R.R., Kallgren, C.A.: A focus theory of normative conduct: Recycling the concept of norms to reduce littering in public places. Journal of Personality and Social Psychology 58(6), 1015 (1990)
5. Davidsson, P.: Agent based social simulation: a computer science view. Journal of Artificial Societies and Social Simulation 5 (2002)
6. DeJong, W., Schneider, S.K., Towvim, L.G., Murphy, M.J., Doerr, E.E., Simonsen, N.R., Mason, K.E., Scribner, R.A.: A multisite randomized trial of social norms marketing campaigns to reduce college student drinking. Journal of Studies on Alcohol (2006)
7. Elster, J.: Social norms and economic theory. The Journal of Economic Perspectives 3(4), 99–117 (1989)
8. Goldstein, N.J., Cialdini, R.B., Griskevicius, V.: A room with a viewpoint: Using social norms to motivate environmental conservation in hotels. Journal of Consumer Research 35(3), 472–482 (2008)
9. Habermas, J.: The Theory of Communicative Action: Reason and the Rationalization of Society, vol. 1. Beacon Press (1985)
10. Hunt, A.: Social norms and energy conservation. Journal of Public Economics 95(9-10), 1082–1095 (2011); Special Issue: The Role of Firms in Tax Systems
11. Kitts, J.A., Chiang, Y.-S.: Norms. In: Encyclopedia of Social Problems. Sage Publications (2008)
12. Mankoff, J., Matthews, D., Fussell, S.R., Johnson, M.: Leveraging social networks to motivate individuals to reduce their ecological footprints. In: Hawaii International Conference on System Sciences, p. 87a (2007)
13. Pazzani, M.J.: A framework for collaborative, content-based and demographic filtering. Artificial Intelligence Review 13(5), 393–408 (1999)
14. Reno, R.R., Cialdini, R.B., Kallgren, C.A.: The transsituational influence of social norms. Journal of Personality and Social Psychology 64(1), 104 (1993)
15. Ringold, D.J.: Boomerang effects in response to public health interventions: Some unintended consequences in the alcoholic beverage market. Journal of Consumer Policy 25, 27–63 (2002)
16. Savarimuthu, B.T.R., Cranefield, S.: Norm creation, spreading and emergence: A survey of simulation models of norms in multi-agent systems. Multiagent and Grid Systems 7(1), 21–54 (2011)
17. Schultz, P.W.: Changing behavior with normative feedback interventions: A field experiment on curbside recycling. Basic and Applied Social Psychology 21(1), 25–36 (1999)
18. Schultz, P.W., Nolan, J.M., Cialdini, R.B., Goldstein, N.J., Griskevicius, V.: The constructive, destructive, and reconstructive power of social norms. Psychological Science 18(5), 429 (2007)
19. Smajgl, A., Izquierdo, L.R., Huigen, M.: Modeling endogenous rule changes in an institutional context: The adico sequence. Advances in Complex Systems (ACS) 11(02), 199–215 (2008)
20. Smajgl, A., Izquierdo, L.R., Huigen, M.: Rules, knowledge and complexity: How agents shape their institutional environment. Journal of Modelling and Simulation of Systems 1(2), 98–107 (2010)

# An Agent-Based Model
# of Stereotype Communication

Jens Pfau, Michael Kirley, and Yoshihisa Kashima

The University of Melbourne
Parkville, Victoria 3010, Australia
{jpfau,mkirley,ykashima}@unimelb.edu.au

**Abstract.** We introduce an agent-based model of the communication of
stereotype-relevant communication. The model takes into account that
the communication of information related to a particular stereotype is
governed by the actual and the perceived sharedness of this stereotype.
To this end, agents in this model are capable of representing which
stereotype-relevant information their communication partners hold. We
estimate the parameters of this model with empirical data. The model
is a step towards an understanding of how stereotypes are formed and
maintained during inter-personal communication as a function of factors
such as the social network that underlies this communication.

**Keywords:** Agent-based Modeling, Connectionist Modeling,
Stereotypes.

## 1 Introduction

*Stereotypes* can be understood as characteristics that are attributed to all members of a social group. While stereotypes support us in the navigation of our
complex social environment, they are also related to undesirable effects such as
prejudicing and the derogation and discrimination of out-groups [23]. Therefore
stereotypes can be an eminent threat to social sustainability. Social psychology—
the science that studies how we make sense of our social environment—has spent
much effort on studying the intra-personal cognitive processes that influence the
activation and application of stereotypes [22].

However, information about members of other social groups is clearly not
so often acquired first-hand through direct contact but more often second-hand
through inter-personal communication. In the wider context of a social
community, inter-personal communication of stereotype-relevant information
manipulates the state of stereotypes within that community. In fact, this communication typically serves the maintenance of stereotypes, which ensures that
they are rather stable over time [13]. This calls for a two-fold research program:
First, one needs to gain an understanding of the mechanisms that govern the
exchange of stereotype-relevant information during inter-personal communication. Second, given this understanding, one needs to study how on the larger
scale inter-personal communication adds up to the formation and maintenance

S. Cranefield and I. Song (Eds.): PRIMA 2011 Workshops, LNAI 7580, pp. 32–47, 2012.

of stereotypes. Recently, research has started to focus on the first part of this agenda [4,12,14,27] and some discussion has been initiated on the second part [13]. We see potential for agent-based modeling to contribute to this second part: Agent-based modeling allows the direct representation and simulation of actors and their interactions with the possibility of considering a large population of actors [9]. Hence, agent-based modeling is predestined for drawing on the results of the first part of this agenda to enable an analysis targeting the second part.

We introduce an agent-based model of the communication of stereotype-relevant information. The model is based on an empirical study by Lyons and Kashima on the communication of *stereotype-consistent* (SC) and *stereotype-inconsistent* (SI) information through a chain of communicators [14]. Consider a stereotype "All members of group G are smart". SC information would then be, for example, "A, a member of G, is smart/clever/intelligent". SI information would be, for example, "A, a member of G, is stupid/unintelligent".

Lyons and Kashima found that the extent to which either SC or SI information is communicated depends on whether relevant stereotypes are actually shared between the communicators and whether they are perceived to be shared. Assuming that stereotypes are typically perceived to be shared with close friends or family but not with others, these results suggest that the exchange of stereotype-relevant information along strong ties in the social network is different from the exchange along weak ties [13]. This highlights the role of the social network in the diffusion process and motivates the application of agent-based models that account for the structure of the underlying social network.

Taking the results of Lyons and Kashima into account, our model enables agents to create an internal representation of the information they as well as third parties associate with other individuals or social groups. Following the recent development of computational modeling in social psychology [20], we rely on a distributed *connectionist model* for the representation of memory. This architecture allows the integrated storage and retrieval of information about individuals and groups.

Our model provides a perspective for studying how the communication of stereotype-relevant information might play out in larger societies, also as a function of the underlying social network. The model takes into consideration that individuals obtain information about others first- as well as second-hand and make varying assumptions about the stereotypes held by their communication partners. Existing computational models of stereotyping do not appear to represent these details appropriately. They are either restricted to intra-personal cognitive processes [16,21,26] or represent communication and the storage of information about others in limiting and unintuitive ways [24,25].

We begin by introducing the experiments and results of Lyons and Kashima. Then we discuss existing agent-based models of stereotype communication. We introduce our model and describe a procedure for estimating the parameters of this model. We rely on an evolutionary algorithm to find those parameters under which the model best reproduces the empirical data obtained by Lyons and Kashima. We present our results and conclude the paper with a brief discussion.

## 2  Experiments by Lyons and Kashima

In this section, we describe the experiments of Lyons and Kashima and briefly present their results. This information is essential for the specification of our model and for the estimation of its parameters. Lyons and Kashima try to answer the question how *actual sharedness* and *perceived sharedness* of stereotypes is conducive to an *SC bias*—a preference for communicating SC information.

Lyons and Kashima rely on an experimental paradigm known as the serial reproduction chain to study the communication of stereotype-relevant information [1]. Subjects are grouped into chains of four and are individually primed with background (stereotype) information about a fictional group, the *Jamayans*. Subsequently, a story about *Jay*, a particular Jamayan, is communicated through the chains. Every subject reads and memorizes a version of the story reproduced by the previous subject and then reproduces this story for the next subject in the chain. The clue is that the story about Jay consists partly of SC information and partly of SI information with regard to the stereotype about the Jamayans previously learnt by the subjects. At every position in the chain, the proportion of SC and SI content retained from the original story is measured, which indicates to which extent communication favors SC over SI information.

To study the influence of actual and perceived stereotype sharedness, a $2 \times 2$ factorial experimental design is constructed with two factors:

**Actual sharedness.** All subjects in the chain are either primed with the same information about the Jamayans (*shared condition*) or the second and fourth subjects in the chain are primed with information that is contradictory to the one that the first and third subjects are primed with (*unshared condition*).

**Perceived sharedness.** All subjects in the chain are either told (*knowledge condition*) or not (*ignorance condition*) that the next person in the chain (the *audience*) has learnt the same information about the Jamayans.

This yields four experimental conditions. Each of these is represented by 8 serial reproduction chains of 4 subjects each. The following summary data is reported, summing up to 30 data points:

- Overall proportion of *SC and SI* content reproduced.
- Proportion of *SC and SI* content reproduced in the *knowledge* condition.
- Proportion of *SC and SI* content reproduced in the *ignorance* condition.
- Proportion of *SC and SI* content reproduced in the *shared* condition.
- Proportion of *SC and SI* content reproduced in the *unshared* condition.
- Proportion of content reproduced at every position in the chains.
- Proportion of *SC and SI* content reproduced in the *shared* condition at every position in the chain.
- Proportion of *SC and SI* content reproduced in the *unshared* condition at every position in the chain.

Lyons and Kashima find that an SC bias emerges only when the stereotype is shared by all subjects in the chain and subjects believe that their audience is ignorant of the stereotype (shared-ignorance condition). This result is explained in terms of Grice's *maxims of quality and quantity* [10]. In general, subjects rely on their stereotype as truthful information (maxim of quality) when assessing and interpreting perceived information. Hence, SC information is favored over SI information. When the audience is deemed unaware of the stereotype (ignorance condition), SC information is also assumed to be informative (maxim of quantity), which contributes further to the SC bias. However, when the audience is assumed to have knowledge of the stereotype (knowledge condition), SI information is more informative and an SC bias fails to emerge.

## 3    Connectionist Models of Stereotype Communication

This section gives a brief introduction into connectionist modeling and existing connectionist agent-based models of the communication of stereotype-relevant information. The basic elements of a connectionist model are a set of processing *units* connected by *weighted links* reminiscent of neurons and synapses respectively. The state of every unit is described by its *activation* level, which is determined by the input received from other units via incoming links and an *activation function* applied to this input. Computation then proceeds by propagating externally applied activation through the network.

The purpose of such a network is the learning and reproduction of external activation patterns. Learning relies on incremental changes to the weights between units in the network. The weights of the network are often equated with long-term memory and the current activation levels within the network with short-term memory. Thus connectionism lends itself to the modeling of human memory and cognition, essentially blurring the distinction between storage and processing. This approach was pioneered by Rumelhart and McClelland [18].

A distinction is made between so called *localist representations*, in which each unit corresponds to a particular concept, and *distributed representations*, in which no particular meaning is given to individual units but to patterns of activation over these units. An advantage of distributed representations is that the degree of similarity between two concepts is encoded in the similarity of the activation patterns they are associated with. This allows the network to learn prototype representations from exemplars with similar activation patterns and to process new exemplars according to their similarity with the previously extracted prototypes [19]. This characteristic makes distributed connectionist models well suited for the modeling of stereotyping processes.

For the modeling of stereotyping, so called *fully recurrent networks* have proven useful [16,21,26]. In these networks, all units provide input to all other units. Models of stereotype communication that are based on this particular connectionist architecture were introduced by Van Overwalle and Heylighen [24] and Van Rooy [25], whereby the latter work is based on the former. Because Van Overwalle and Heylighen show how their model can reproduce the experiments of Lyons and Kashima, we focus our discussion on their work. In their model, every agent consists of a fully recurrent network with a localist representation. The 5 units of each network represent the concepts "Jamayans", "honest" and "smart" (SC), "dishonest" and "stupid" (SI). Each agent is hence able to learn and reproduce the association between the Jayamans and SC and SI information.

Communication between different agents is represented by the flow of activation along connections that link units of the agents that represent the same concepts. Connections are annotated with so-called trust weights in each direction, reflecting how much the receiving agent trusts in the sending agent with regard to the particular concept and vice versa. The weight an agent gives to activation received via such a connection is determined by the receiving trust weight of that connection (maxim of quality). A sending agent attenuates activation sent along a connection if the sending trust weight is high and boosts the activation otherwise (maxim of quantity).

The model of Van Overwalle and Heylighen reproduces the results of Lyons and Kashima to a good degree. In an initial learning phase, agents are primed with the association between the Jamayans and the SC information. In the second phase, agents communicate an association between the Jamayans and SC as well as SI information through the chain, reflecting the content of the story about Jay. However, we see room for improvement, both with regard to the architecture and to the reproduction of the experiments:

- The simulations of Van Overwalle and Heylighen do not properly represent the $2 \times 2$ experimental design of Lyon and Kashima. Their shared-ignorance and unshared-ignorance simulations are inappropriately compared to the data of the shared and unshared conditions of Lyons and Kashima, which actually also include the shared-knowledge and unshared-knowledge conditions respectively. Their shared-ignorance and shared-knowledge simulations are then inappropriately compared to the data of the knowledge and ignorance conditions, which actually also include the unshared-ignorance and unshared-knowledge conditions respectively.
- There is no distinction made between the Jamayans and Jay, and the story about Jay has essentially the meaning of a story about the Jamayans. Yet an important capability of human memory and cognition is the integration of information about individuals and prototypes or stereotypes.
- The representation of what an agent believes another agent to believe in terms of trust weights is neat to some extent but unintuitive. A more direct representation would consider this information to be part of the agent's memory and hence stored in the network itself.

# 4   An Agent-Based Model of Stereotype Communication

This section describes an agent-based model that enables the simulation of the communication of stereotype-relevant information. Our description is informal to make it accessible to a wider audience.[1] We start our discussion with an overview of the model and then go into the details.

## 4.1   Overview

The previous discussion provides the requirements for the model: Agents need to be able to learn who associates which information with whom. In the experiments of Lyons and Kashima, every subject stores and retrieves what they themselves as well as the next person in the chain (audience) believe about the Jamayans and Jay. Hence these associations consist of three elements: a *subject*, a *target*, and the *content* that the subject associates with the target. Subject and target can correspond to any arbitrary individual or social group, e.g. the *self* or the audience in case of the subject and the Jamayans or Jay in the case of the target. Both for the subject and the target, the ability to represent similarity between different individuals or groups is essential. For example, Jay is not an isolated individual but perceived as a member of the Jamayans. Memory should only be responsible for storage and recall of information but not be intertwined with the interactions between agents. The content is what is communicated, subject to adjustment according to the maxims of quality and quantity. Here, we consider content to consist of the extent to which it carries SC and SI information.

## 4.2   Memory Storage and Reproduction

Following previous models of stereotyping processes, we rely on a fully recurrent network as the representation of memory. However, our model is distinguished by two features: We enable the network to encode the triadic associations of subject, target, and content described above; and we adopt a network model that allows for hidden units. *Hidden units* are not part of the patterns to be learnt and reproduced but allow the network to create an internal representation of the associations to be learnt. This improves the expressiveness of the network. Figure 1 illustrates this architecture. The network consists of four pools of units for subject, target, content, and hidden units. To enable the simultaneous integration of exemplars and prototypes, we assume that subject and target concepts are described by a distributed representation. For the sake of simplicity, SC and SI content units assume a localist representation. The extent to which these two units are activated when a particular subject-target pattern is provided represents how much the subject associates the target with SC and SI information. However, SC and SI are only labels and their meaning could be replaced by anything else. Activation values of all units are in the range $[0, 1]$.

## 4.3   Network Processing

We base the network processing—propagation of activation and learning of network weights—on the *recurrent back-propagation* network and learning algorithm

---

[1] For those interested in details, the source code of these simulations and instructions on how to reproduce our results can be found here:
`http://www.csse.unimelb.edu.au/~pfauj/absss2011/`.

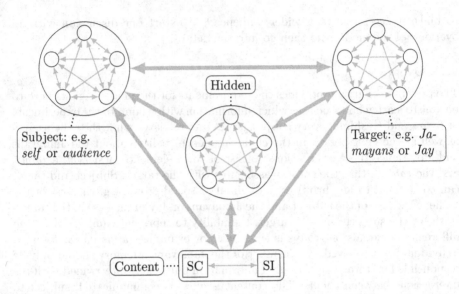

**Fig. 1.** An illustration of the network architecture of the model. The units of the network are grouped into four pools: subject, target, content, and hidden units. The network is fully recurrent, i.e. every unit provides input to every other unit. While the units in the subject and target pools adhere to a distributed representation, the units in the content pool take a localist representation.

described by McClelland [15], which has been used for example in modeling the processing of semantic memory [17]. Refer to Williams and Zipser for a comprehensive review on recurrent back-propagation [28]. In contrast to the networks and learning algorithms used in previous connectionist models of stereotyping processes, this architecture enables learning for networks with hidden units.

Processing includes a *forward pass* and a *backward pass* and subsequent weight updates. During the forward pass, external input is applied to some of the units and propagated through the network by iteratively updating the activation of all units over a number of *ticks*. At the same time, some units can be provided with a *target* activation. For every tick a unit is provided with a target, the *error* between the target and the current activation of this unit is recorded. Typically, an input pattern is provided during the first ticks and a target pattern during the last ticks. In general, however, inputs and targets can be applied at any ticks and can vary between different ticks. During the backward pass, errors are "back-propagated through time", i.e. through all the ticks of the forward pass and through all links between units, to calculate overall errors. Based on these errors, the weights between units are updated subject to a learning rate $\epsilon$. With sufficient learning of an input-target pattern, providing the input pattern will cause the network to reproduce the target pattern. The ticks of the forward pass are partitioned into a number of intervals such that all intervals consist of the same number of ticks. From here on, we refer to intervals instead of ticks.

## 4.4   Communication

Having described how agents are able to store and retrieve associations between subject, target, and content (SC and SI information), we now establish how they actually communicate. Communication knows two sides: the one of the sending agent and the one of the receiving agent. Within the context of this paper, we assume that it is $(SC, SI)$ tuples with $SC, SI \in [0, 1]$ that are communicated between agents. The value of such a tuple describes to which extent the communication contains SC and SI information. This maps onto the data measured by Lyons and Kashima. Next, we need to describe how an agent determines the $(SC, SI)$ tuple to communicate to another agent, and how a receiving agent integrates such a tuple into its memory.

**Sending.** A sending agent recalls the SC and SI information it associates with a particular target by reproducing that information from memory. To do so, the agent activates the subject and target units with an activation pattern consisting of a part that represents the agent itself and a part that represents that particular target. The pattern is used as an input for a number of intervals. Then the input is removed and the network is allowed to settle over a number of further intervals. The activation found at the SC and SI units represents the extent to which the agent itself associates the target with SC and SI information. We denote this tuple by $(SC_{self}, SI_{self})$.

We highlighted previously that people adjust the information they communicate to their audience in line with the maxim of quantity. Therefore, the agent also reproduces the SC and SI information that the audience associates with the target. The procedure is essentially the one above, yet the subject units are activated with a pattern that represents the audience. We denote this tuple by $(SC_{audience}, SI_{audience})$.

The $(SC_{com}, SI_{com})$ tuple the agent communicates is then determined by an interpretation of the maxim of quantity as follows:

$$SC_{com} = SC_{self} - SC_{self} * (1 - SI_{audience}) * SI_{self} * \beta_{quantity}$$
$$SI_{com} = SI_{self} - SI_{self} * (1 - SC_{audience}) * SC_{self} * \beta_{quantity}$$

Both equations are symmetrical. The communication of each type of information is reduced inversely proportionally to what the audience is assumed to know about the other type of information and proportionally to how much the agent associates the target with the other type of information. The reduction is adjusted by a parameter $\beta_{quantity}$. This means that the more the audience is assumed to know about one type of information, the more the agent talks about the other, providing information novel to the audience. Also, the less an agent is able to talk about one type of information, the more it talks about the other.

**Receiving.** We discussed previously that people turn to their stereotypes or in fact their prior knowledge when assessing information that they receive. So on receiving SC and SI information about a particular target, the agent first reproduces the information it associates with that target itself. This follows the same procedure as above, yielding a tuple $(SC_{self}, SI_{self})$. Based on that, the $(SC_{com}, SI_{com})$ tuple received is corrected towards this information as follows:

$$SC = SC_{com} + (SC_{self} - SC_{com}) * |SC_{self} - SC_{com}| * \beta_{quality}$$
$$SI = SI_{com} + (SI_{self} - SI_{com}) * |SI_{self} - SI_{com}| * \beta_{quality}$$

Thus, the information received is made more similar to the one reproduced from memory. After this adjustment, the agent learns the information. To do so, the agent provides an input pattern to the subject and target units that consists of a part representing the agent itself and a part representing the target. After a few intervals, the input is removed and the network allowed to cycle freely for a number of intervals. Then the $(SC, SI)$ tuple is provided as a target for the last few intervals. Finally, weights are updated subject to recorded errors.

## 5    Parameter Estimation

In this section, we describe the parameter estimation of the model using the data of Lyons and Kashima. We describe how our model is set up to reflect their experimental conditions. Then we provide the details of an evolutionary algorithm used to find parameter values for our model that yield simulations with an outcome close to the empirical data. Finally, we present our results.

### 5.1    Experimental Setup

We represent each serial reproduction chain in the experiments of Lyons and Kashima by 4 agents arranged in a row. All agents undergo an initial learning phase, in which they learn to associate the self with the Jamayans and a particular $(SC, SI)$ tuple as well as the audience with the Jamayans and a particular $(SC, SI)$ tuple. Every agent makes use of its own particular patterns for the self, the audience, and the Jamayans but this is not of importance here. Essential is that the $(SC, SI)$ tuples learnt differ by the experimental condition of the chain the agent belongs to and its position within that chain. Table 1 demonstrates the patterns learnt by the agents in the different conditions and positions.

The patterns are learnt alternately over a number of learning iterations. For every pattern, an input activation is provided to the network consisting of a subject and a target pattern for a number of intervals before it is removed. Then the network is allowed to cycle freely for some intervals, and finally the target pattern consisting of a particular $(SC, SI)$ tuple is provided for a number of intervals. Then weight updates are performed based on recorded errors. For each of the 4 experimental conditions we consider 8 such chains. The chains differ by the random initialization of network weights of the agents.

The transmission of the story through the chain proceeds as follows. The first agent receives an $(SC, SI)$ tuple of $(1, 1)$ to reflect that the story consists of an

**Table 1.** An overview of the patterns that agents learn in the priming phase of the different experimental conditions. Every tuple in the cells consists of two tuples: One representing a distributed input pattern of activation over the subject and target units, and one localist target pattern over the content (SC and SI) units. S and A stand for patterns of activation corresponding to the self and the audience respectively. J stands for a pattern of activation corresponding to the Jamayans. In the shared-ignorance condition, for example, all agents learn to associate the self with the Jamayans and SC information but not SI information. They also learn to associate the audience with the Jamayans with no SC or SI information.

|  | shared condition | unshared condition |
|---|---|---|
| ignorance condition | Agents 1-4: [(S,J),(1,0)] [(A,J),(0,0)] | Agents 1,3: [(S,J),(1,0)] [(A,J),(0,0)] |
|  |  | Agents 2,4: [(S,J),(0,1)] [(A,J),(0,0)] |
| knowledge condition | Agents 1-4: [(S,J),(1,0)] [(A,J),(1,0)] | Agents 1,3: [(S,J),(1,0)] [(A,J),(1,0)] |
|  |  | Agents 2,4: [(S,J),(0,1)] [(A,J),(0,1)] |

equal proportion of SC and SI information. The agent learns to associate this information with the self and Jay. Jay is represented by a pattern over the target units that has some overlap with the pattern of the Jamayans. This represents that Jay is perceived as a Jamayan. The number of learning iterations here is $\frac{2}{3}$ times the one used for learning the background information about the Jamayans. This is the proportion between the relevant content in the report about the Jamayans and the content in the story about Jay used in the experiments of Lyons and Kashima. The agent then reproduces the information with the audience in mind as described in Section 4, yielding an $(SC, SI)$ tuple. The next agent in the chain receives this information, stores and reproduces it, and so forth. We record the communicated $(SC, SI)$ tuples at all positions in the chains as representative of the SC and SI content reproduced.

## 5.2   Evolutionary Algorithm

*Evolutionary algorithms* are a tool for parameter optimization [8]. Here, we reformulate parameter estimation as an optimization problem with the objective of finding a parameter $\hat{\theta}$ that minimizes a distance function $d(D_{obs}, D_\theta)$ between the observed data $D_{obs}$ and the data $D_\theta$ produced by the model under parameter $\theta$. Evolutionary algorithms are a useful tool for parameter estimation when the relationship between parameters and dependent variables is complex such that an analytical solution for $\hat{\theta}$ is unavailable, and when the parameter space is large such that an exhaustive enumeration of all possible parameters in order to find $\hat{\theta}$ is unachievable. These characteristics often apply to agent-based models, which is why evolutionary algorithms have been applied, for instance, to estimate the

**Table 2.** A list of all parameters of the model. Some parameters have fixed values, others are provided with a set of possible values from which the evolutionary algorithm can create parameters.

| Parameter | Description | Set of possible values |
|---|---|---|
| $\theta^1$ | Number of iterations for learning background knowledge about Jamayans | $\Theta^1 = \{10, 20, 50, 100, 200, 500,$ $800, 1000, 1500, 2000\}$ |
| $\theta^2$ | Learning rate $\epsilon$ | $\Theta^2 = [0,1] \subset \mathbb{R}$ |
| $\theta^3$ | Strength of maxim of quality $\beta_{quality}$ | $\Theta^3 = [0,1] \subset \mathbb{R}$ |
| $\theta^4$ | Strength of maxim of quantity $\beta_{quantity}$ | $\Theta^4 = [0,1] \subset \mathbb{R}$ |
| $\theta^5$ | Number of hidden units in the network | $\Theta^5 = \{0, 1, 5, 10, 20, 40, 50\}$ |
| $\theta^6$ | Proportion of units in the patterns of the Jamayans and Jay that overlap | $\Theta^6 = \{0.5\}$ |
| $\theta^7$ | Number of units for the subject and target pools | $\Theta^s = \{20\}$ |
| $\theta^8$ | Number of intervals for all patterns | $\Theta^7 = \{7\}$ |
| $\theta^9$ | Number of ticks per interval for all patterns | $\Theta^8 = \{4\}$ |
| $\theta^{10}$ | Number of initial intervals of the $\theta^8$ intervals during which any input pattern is provided | $\Theta^{10} = \{3\}$ |
| $\theta^{11}$ | Number of last intervals of the $\theta^8$ intervals during which any target pattern is provided | $\Theta^{11} = \{2\}$ |

parameters of agent-based models of financial markets [5], marine ecosystems [7], and retail markets [11].

The evolutionary algorithm uses a *population* of $\mu = 50$ candidate parameters $(\theta_1, \ldots, \theta_\mu)$ randomly generated from a set $\Theta$ of possible parameters. Every parameter $\theta_i$ is a vector $(\theta_i^1, \ldots, \theta_i^n)$ of multiple entries $\theta_i^j$, each standing for one of the model parameters introduced previously. Table 2 lists all model parameters $\theta^j$ and their sets of possible values $\Theta^j$. Some model parameters are fixed, the first 5 are not. Hence, for the purpose of parameter optimization each parameter $\theta_i$ is a tuple $(\theta_i^1, \ldots, \theta_i^5)$ and the set of possible parameters $\Theta = \Theta^1 \times \cdots \times \Theta^5$ is the set of all possible tuples. The value of parameter $\theta_6$ is fixed to 0.5 reflecting that a reasonable assumption is that Jay is perceived to be in equal proportions an individual and a Jamayan group member (in the story about Jay, half of the items are stereotype-consistent, half of the items are stereotype-inconsistent). The values of parameters $\theta^8$ to $\theta^{11}$ are set based on previous work [17].

In each of 100 generations, $\lambda = 20$ offsprings are created by *recombination* from parent parameters chosen from the population, offsprings are *mutated*, and then those $\mu$ best performing parent or offspring parameters are *selected* and retained to form the next generation.

For every offspring, $\rho = 2$ parent parameters are selected randomly from the population. The offspring parameter is created by randomly selecting each entry in its parameter vector from either of the parents. Mutation distinguishes between those entries in the offspring's parameter vector holding discrete values and those entries holding continuous values. Discrete-valued entries are mutated by randomly retaining the current value or selecting the next largest or smallest value in the set defining all possible values for that parameter entry (see Table 2). Continuous-valued entries are mutated by adding normally distributed random noise $\mathcal{N}(0, \sigma_g)$ to the current value, where $\sigma_g$ depends on the current generation $g$. We set $\sigma_1 = 1.0$ and $\sigma_g = 0.99 * \sigma_{g-1}$. Thus, the precision of the evolutionary algorithm with respect to continuous-valued entries in the parameter vector increases with each generation.

During selection, those $\mu$ parent or offspring parameters $\theta$ that produce the minimal values for $d(D_{obs}, D_\theta)$, are selected and retained for the next generation. The empirical data $D_{obs}$ is comprised of the 30 data points described in Section 2. The data $D_\theta$ is obtained by creating an experimental setup as described in the previous section, simulating the model under parameter $\theta$, and obtaining the same 30 summary statistics as Lyons and Kashima. The distance function $d(D_{obs}, D_\theta)$ is defined as $1 - r^2(D_{obs}, D_\theta)$ where $r^2(D_{obs}, D_\theta)$ is the squared correlation coefficient between $D_{obs}$ and $D_\theta$. We are not interested in an exact reproduction of the empirical data but in reproducing the pattern of the data.

## 5.3  Results

The best performing parameter found by the optimization method produced an $r^2$ value of 0.96. Repeated executions of this optimization also yielded best $r^2$ with $0.95 < r^2 < 0.96$.

Figure 2 shows the distribution of parameter values for those 81 parameters that yielded $r^2 \geq 0.95$. The values of the best performing parameter are marked with a vertical line in each plot. The number of learning iterations ($\theta^1$) is generally high, which indicates slow learning. The bulk of the learning rate $\epsilon$ ($\theta^2$) at the lower end of the scale is in line with previous research. Larger values of $\epsilon$ usually enable faster learning but also might cause instabilities that need to be compensated for by adjustments to the learning procedure [18]. Examples of such adjustments are the decay of weights over time or a momentum term so that weight updates are influenced by earlier updates in addition to the current one. However, further investigations, which are not presented in detail here because of space restrictions, have shown that those parameters with a larger $\epsilon$ perform best when validated against another data set. The strength of the maxim of quality $\beta_{quality}$ ($\theta^3$) shows the smallest spread relative to the considered range. Apparently, the model is more sensitive to this parameter than to the others. The strength of the maxim of quantity $\beta_{quantity}$ ($\theta^4$) extends over a range of about 0.5. The number of hidden units ($\theta^5$) is substantial in most parameters.

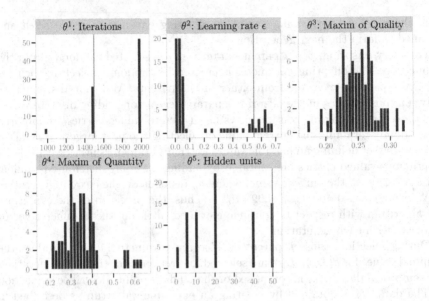

**Fig. 2.** Distribution of parameter values for all parameters created during the evolutionary algorithm that yielded $r^2$ values $\geq 0.95$. Vertical lines mark the parameter values of the parameter that yielded the best $r^2$ value.

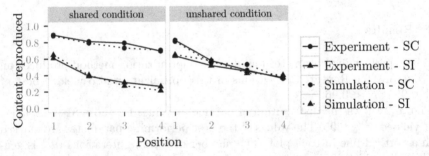

**Fig. 3.** SC and SI content reproduced in the shared and unshared conditions at different positions in the chain

In fact, among these parameters there is none without any hidden units, which suggests a crucial role for hidden units.

Figures 3 and 4 show the regression-adjusted results of the best performing parameter plotted onto the results of the experiment of Lyons and Kashima. These are in fact the plots presented by them apart from the aggregation of different story zones we conducted here. Obviously, the match between simulation and experimental data is within a reasonable error. We take that the model is generally capable of reproducing the results of Lyons and Kashima.

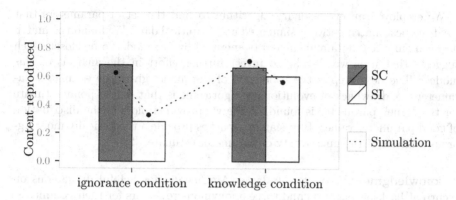

**Fig. 4.** Overall SC and SI content reproduced in the ignorance and knowledge conditions

# 6    Discussion and Conclusions

We have presented an agent-based model for the investigation of the relationship between actual and perceived sharedness of stereotypes and the communication of stereotype-relevant information. Our model has two key features: a) Agents hold a representation not only of the information they (subject) associate with other individuals or groups (target) but also of the information others (subject) associate with third parties (target); b) The representations of subjects and targets allow overlap between different individuals or groups so that learning or recalling information about one individual always happens in light of the information stored about similar others. We have identified these two features as crucial for models of stereotype communication.

Our agent model relies on a connectionist architecture as a representation of memory. A simple communication mechanism allows the exchange of stereotype-relevant information in terms of the degree to which this information is stereotype-consistent or -inconsistent. Our work stands in the tradition of other approaches to the modeling of stereotyping processes in psychological literature. We have not drawn on any approaches to communication between goal-directed agents, such as speech acts as rational action [6] or argumentation dialogues [3]. The reason for this is that the information exchange our model represents is one-way and does not involve any complex form of dialogue. Also, a complex communication protocol would impede the scaling of this model to larger agent populations.

This work enables the development of agent-based models of stereotype communication in which agents from different groups can learn about each other or third parties not only first-hand but also second-hand by communication. This supports the investigation of how stereotype-relevant information diffuses through different networks and in which conditions first-hand experience could overcome the stereotype-maintaining force of second-hand information exchange.

We employed an evolutionary algorithm to find the set of parameters that yield the best match between simulated and empirical data. We found the match between empirical data and the data generated by our model to be close, which suggests that it is worthwhile to invest further effort in the analysis of this model.[2] The next step is the validation of the model given the estimated parameters. A drawback of evolutionary algorithms is that only a point estimate for the "true" parameter is found. While we provided plots of the distribution of good parameter values, Bayesian approaches provide a theoretically more rigorous analysis of the uncertainty of parameter estimates [2].

**Acknowledgments.** We thank James McClelland for helpful discussions on recurrent back-propagation and three anonymous reviewers for their comments.

# References

1. Bartlett, F.C.: Remembering: A study in experimental and social psychology. Cambridge University Press, Cambridge (1932)
2. Beaumont, M.: Approximate bayesian computation in evolution and ecology. Annual Review of Ecology, Evolution, and Systematics 41(1), 379–406 (2010)
3. Bench-Capon, T.J.M., Dunne, P.E.: Argumentation in artificial intelligence. Artificial Intelligence 171(10-15), 619–641 (2007)
4. Brauer, M., Judd, C.M., Jacquelin, V.: The communication of social stereotypes: The effects of group discussion and information distribution on stereotypic appraisals. Journal of Personality and Social Psychology 81(3), 463–475 (2001)
5. Caporale, G.M., Serguieva, A., Wu, H.: Financial contagion: Evolutionary optimisation of a multinational agent-based model. CESifo Working Paper Series 2444, CESifo Group Munich (2008)
6. Cohen, P.R., Levesque, H.J.: Rational interaction as the basis for communication. In: Cohen, P.R., Morgan, J., Pollack, M.E. (eds.) Intentions in Communication, ch. 12, pp. 221–256. MIT Press, Cambridge (1990)
7. Duboz, R., Versmisse, D., Travers, M., Ramat, E., Shin, Y.: Application of an evolutionary algorithm to the inverse parameter estimation of an individual-based model. Ecological Modelling 221(5), 840–849 (2010)
8. Eiben, A.E., Smith, J.E.: Introduction to Evolutionary Computing. Springer, Heidelberg (2003)
9. Gilbert, N.: Agent-based models. Sage Publications, London (2008)
10. Grice, H.P.: Logic and conversation. In: Cole, P., Morgan, J.L. (eds.) Syntax and Semantics 3: Speech Acts. Academic Press, New York (1975)
11. Heppenstall, A.J., Evans, A.J., Birkin, M.H.: Genetic algorithm optimisation of an agent-based model for simulating a retail market. Environment and Planning B: Planning and Design 34(6), 1051–1070 (2007)
12. Kurz, T., Lyons, A.: Intergroup influences on the stereotype consistency bias in communication: Does it matter who we are communicating about and to whom we are communicating? Social Cognition 27(6), 893–904 (2009)

---

[2] We note that a comparison between the performance of our model and the one of Van Overwalle and Heylighen [24] in reproducing the experiments of Lyons and Kashima [14] is not meaningful because their experimental setup does not match the one of Lyons and Kashima appropriately as discussed in Section 3.

13. Lyons, A., Clark, A., Kashima, Y., Kurz, T.: Cultural dynamics of stereotypes: Social network processes and the perpetuation of stereotypes. In: Kashima, Y., Fieldler, K., Freytag, P. (eds.) Stereotype Dynamics: Language-Based Approaches to the Formation, Maintenance, and Transformation of Stereotypes, pp. 59–92. Lawrence Erlbaum Associates (2007)
14. Lyons, A., Kashima, Y.: How are stereotypes maintained through communication? The influence of stereotype sharedness. Journal of Personality and Social Psychology 85(6), 989–1005 (2003)
15. McClelland, J.L.: Explorations in Parallel Distributed Processing: A Handbook of Models, Programs, and Exercises, 2nd edn. (2011)
16. Queller, S., Smith, E.R.: Subtyping versus bookkeeping in stereotype learning and change: Connectionist simulations and empirical findings. Journal of Personality and Social Psychology 82(3), 300–313 (2002)
17. Rogers, T.T., Lambon Ralph, M.A., Garrard, P., Bozeat, S., McClelland, J.L., Hodges, J.R., Patterson, K.: The structure and deterioration of semantic memory: A neuropsychological and computational investigation. Psychological Review 111, 205–235 (2004)
18. Rumelhart, D.E., McClelland, J.L.: the PDP Research Group: Parallel Distributed Processing. MIT Press, Cambridge (1986)
19. Smith, E.R.: What do connectionism and social psychology offer each other? Journal of Personality and Social Psychology 70(5), 893–912 (1996)
20. Smith, E.R.: Distributed connectionist models in social psychology. Social and Personality Psychology Compass 3(1), 64–76 (2009)
21. Smith, E.R., DeCoster, J.: Knowledge acquisition, accessibility, and use in person perception and stereotyping: Simulation with a recurrent connectionist network. Journal of Personality and Social Psychology 74(1), 21–35 (1998)
22. Stangor, C.: The study of stereotyping, prejudice, and discrimination within social psychology: A quick history of theory and research. In: Nelson, T. (ed.) Handbook of Prejudice, Stereotyping, and Discrimination, ch. 1, pp. 1–22. Psychology Press (2009)
23. Stephan, W.G., Ybarra, O., Morrisón, K.R.: Intergroup threat theory. In: Nelson, T. (ed.) Handbook of Prejudice, Stereotyping, and Discrimination, ch. 3, pp. 43–59. Psychology Press (2009)
24. Van Overwalle, F., Heylighen, F.: Talking Nets: A multiagent connectionist approach to communication and trust between individuals. Psychological Review 113(3), 606–627 (2006)
25. Van Rooy, D.: Modeling multidirectional, dynamic social influences in social networks. In: Anderssen, R.S., Braddock, R.D., Newham, L.T.H. (eds.) MODSIM 2009 International Congress on Modelling and Simulation (2009)
26. Van Rooy, D., Van Overwalle, F., Vanhoomissen, T., Labiouse, C., French, R.: A recurrent connectionist model of group biases. Psychological Review 110(3), 536–563 (2003)
27. Wigboldus, D.H.J., Spears, R., Semin, G.R.: When do we communicate stereotypes? Influence of the social context on the linguistic expectancy bias. Group Processes & Intergroup Relations 8(3), 215–230 (2005)
28. Williams, R.J., Zipser, D.: Gradient-based learning algorithms for recurrent networks and their computational complexity. In: Chauvin, Y., Rumelhart, D.E. (eds.) Back-propagation: Theory, Architectures and Applications. Lawrence Erlbaum Associates (1995)

# An Approach to Sustainable Electric Power Allocation Using a Multi-round Multi-unit Combinatorial Auction

Naoki Fukuta[1] and Takayuki Ito[2,3]

[1] Shizuoka University,Hamamatsu Shizuoka 4328011, Japan,
fukuta@cs.inf.shizuoka.ac.jp
http://whitebear.cs.inf.shizuoka.ac.jp/
[2] Nagoya Institute of Technology, Gokiso-cho Nagoya 4668555, Japan
[3] Tokyo University, Bunkyo-ku Tokyo 113-0033, Japan

**Abstract.** In this paper, we present a preliminary idea about applying multi-unit combinatorial auctions to an electric power allocation problem when it includes sustainable power sources and it considers guaranteeing stable continuous use of the supplied power. Multi-unit combinatorial auction is a combinatorial auction that has some items that can be seen as indistinguishable. Theoretically, such mechanisms could be applied for dynamic electricity auctions. We try to illustrate how such a mechanism can be applied to the actual electric power allocation problem when we consider the situation that there are sustainable electric power sources and guaranteeing stable continuous use of them. An approximation mechanism has been applied for a large-scale auction problem to overcome its computational intractability.

## 1 Introduction

One of the main issues on using sustainable electric sources is to solve the mismatches of their production availabilities and consumption needs[13][1]. They are dynamically changing in every time, depending on the consumers' context, weather conditions, etc. Furthermore, some may want to use energy produced from sustainable ways rather than generated by ordinary ways. Of course it might be due to their ideological preferences but sometimes it would be even for economical reasons since, for example, having a badge that shows the certificate of using a certain percentage of renewable energy [1] will increase a chance to have their customers.

On the other hand, there are some investigations and innovations on effective and efficient resource allocations among many self-interested attendees. Combinatorial auctions[2], one of the most popular market mechanisms, have a huge effect on electronic markets and political strategies. For example, Sandholm et al.[18] proposed a market mechanism using their innovative combinatorial auction algorithms. Multi-unit combinatorial auctions are expected to be used on

---

[1] e.g., see http://wwf.panda.org/how_you_can_help/
live_green/renewable_energy/

S. Cranefield and I. Song (Eds.): PRIMA 2011 Workshops, LNAI 7580, pp. 48–63, 2012.

many problems that include quantitative or countable items[12]. Combinatorial auctions provide suitable mechanisms for efficient allocation of resources to self-interested attendees[2]. Therefore, many works have been done to utilize combinatorial auction mechanisms for efficient resource allocation. For example, the Federal Communications Commission (FCC) tried to employ combinatorial auction mechanisms for assigning spectrums to companies[14]. Therefore, it is natural to consider applying an auction-based approach to an electricity power usage allocation problem in a situation that various sustainable electric power sources are widely used.

However, a naive auction-based approach will cause some serious problems (e.g., dramatic up and down of prices due to lack of a proper mechanism to stabilize)[17]. Furthermore, in such case, their bidding might be complicated (e.g., a large number of bids would be necessary to represent them) so that it is very difficult to apply it to a large-scale problem.

To overcome those issues, many approaches have been proposed. For example, Zurel et al. proposed a heuristic approach that combines approximation of LP and a local search algorithm[19]. Also we proposed a parallel greedy approach[6], a performance analysis of algorithms[7][3], and its enhancement[8]. Recently, Fukuta proposed a fast approximation mechanism that can be applied to a multi-unit combinatorial auction which has very large amount of bids so that it cannot be easily solved by existing Linear Problem(LP) solvers[5]. Also the mechanism provided a pricing mechanism that is similar to VCG(Vickery-Clarke-Groves) which increases incentives to tell the true valuations for bidders. However, there is little empirical analysis about how such fast approximation mechanism can be applied to the actual electric power allocation problem. Also, there is a need to stabilize its dramatic vibration of prices through the time.

In this paper, we present a preliminary idea about applying multi-unit combinatorial auctions to an electric power allocation problem when it includes sustainable power sources and it considers guaranteeing stable continuous use of the supplied power. Also we briefly analyze how a fast approximation mechanism can be applied to the problem.

## 2   Preliminary

### 2.1   Multi-unit Combinatorial Auctions

Combinatorial auction is an auction that allows bidders to place bids for a combination of items rather than a single item[2]. The winner determination problem on single unit combinatorial auctions is defined as follows[2]: The set of bidders is denoted by $N = 1, \ldots, n$, and the set of items by $M = \{m_1, \ldots, m_k\}$. $|M| = k$. Bundle $S$ is a set of items: $S \subseteq M$. We denote by $v_i(S)$, bidder $i$'s valuation of the combinatorial bid for bundle $S$. An allocation of the items is described by variables $x_i(S) \in \{0,1\}$, where $x_i(S) = 1$ if and only if bidder $i$ wins bundle $S$. An allocation, $x_i(S)$, is feasible if it allocates no item more than once, for all $j \in M$.

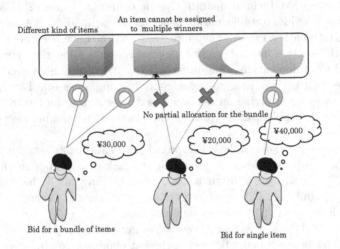

**Fig. 1.** An Example of (Single-Unit) Combinatorial Auction

$$\forall j \in M \ \sum_{i \in N} \sum_{S \ni j} x_i(S) \leq 1$$

The winner determination problem is the problem to maximize total revenue for feasible allocations $X \ni x_i(S)$.

$$\max_{X} \sum_{i \in N} \sum_{S \subseteq M} v_i(S) x_i(S)$$

Fig. 1 shows an example of single-unit combinatorial auction. Note that we used simple *OR-bid* representation as the bidding language. Substitutability can be represented by a set of atomic *OR-bids* with *dummy items*[2]. On *OR-bidding*, each bid can be a winner unless there is a *conflict* with other bids (e.g., the situation in which two bids are placed for the same item but the item can only be assigned to one). To represent substitutability (e.g., a situation that "a bidder wants to have only one of two items"), the bidder can use a virtual item called *dummy item*, which can only be assigned to one bid and can place two *OR-bids* both of which includes the same dummy item in its bundle of items.

When some items in auction can be replaceable each other, i.e., they are indistinguishable, the auction is called multi-unit auction. Multi-unit combinatorial auction is the case when some items are indistinguishable in a combinatorial auction[2].

Multi-unit combinatorial auction can be applied to electricity allocation problems, environmental exhausting right assignment problems, and other problems that considers quantitative or countable items in allocation problem[12].

Essentially, a multi-unit combinatorial auction problem equals to a single-unit combinatorial auction problem when the corresponding bidders treated some items as indistinguishable and placed substitutable bids for those items. Therefore, when we use *OR-bid* representation, a multi-unit combinatorial auction problem can be transformed into a simple single-unit combinatorial auction problem.

However, this expanding approach easily reaches an explosion of bids. For example, when we assume there are three types of item $a$, $b$, and $c$ are auctioned and their stocks are 50, 100, and 200, respectively, a bid for bundle of item $a$, $b$ and $c$ can be expanded to $50 \cdot 100 \cdot 200 = 1,000,000$ of bids. This scale is far from tractable one. Therefore, when we need to have approximate solutions in such situation, it is demanded to realize an approximation algorithm that directly handles a multi-unit combinatorial auction problem.

## 2.2 Extending Lehmann's Approximation Approach

Lehmann's greedy algorithm[11] is a very simple but powerful linear algorithm for winner determination in combinatorial auctions. Here, a bidder declaring $< s, a >$, with $s \subseteq M$ and $a \in \mathcal{R}_+$ will be said to put out a bid $b = < s, a >$. The greedy algorithm can be described as follows. (1) The bids are sorted by some criterion. In [11], Lehmann et al. proposed sorting list $L$ by descending average amount per item. More generally, they proposed sorting $L$ by a criterion of the form $a/|s|^c$ for some number $c$, $c \geq 0$, possibly depending on the number of items, $k$. (2) A greedy algorithm generates an allocation. $L$ is the sorted list in the first phase. Walk down the list $L$, allocates items to bids whose items are still unallocated.

The allocation algorithm can naturally be extended to multi-unit combinatorial auction problems. However, they did not mention about the applicability to multi-unit combinatorial auctions.

In [6],[7], and [8], we have shown that their hill-climbing approach outperforms SA[6], SAT-based algorithms[10], LP-based heuristic approximation approach[19], and a recent LP solver product in the setting when an auction has a massively large number of bids but the given time constraint is very hard. However, the algorithm is designed for single-unit combinatorial auction problems so it cannot be applied for multi-unit problems directly.

## 2.3 Winner Approximation and Pricing

It is crucial for a combinatorial auction mechanism to have proper pricing mechanism. In VCG(Vickery-Clarke-Groves) mechanism, prices that winners will pay will be given as follows[15]. A payment $p_n$ for a winner $n$ is calculated by

$$p_n = \alpha_n - \sum_{i \neq n, S \subseteq M} v_i(S) x_i(S)$$

Here, the right part of the right side of the equation denotes the sum of all bidding prices of won bids, excluding the bids that are placed by the bidder $n$. The left part of the right side of the equation, $\alpha_n$ is defined by

$$\alpha_n = max \sum_{i \neq n, S \subseteq M} v_i(S) x_i(S)$$

for a feasible allocation $X \ni x_i(S)$. This means that the $\alpha_n$ is the sum of all bidding prices of won bids when the allocation is determined as if a bidder $n$ does not place any bids for the auction.

In [15], Nisan et al. showed that optimal allocations should be used for VCG-based pricing to make the auction incentive compatible (i.e., revealing true valuations is the best strategy for each bidders). Also, Lehmann et al. showed that VCG-based pricing with approximate winner determination will not make the auction incentive compatible even when it is assumed that all bidders are single-minded(i.e., each bidder can only place single bid at each auction)[11].

To overcome this issue, Lehmann et al. prepared a special pricing mechanism that can only be applied for their approximate greedy winner determination[11]. However, this pricing mechanism can only be applied to their allocation algorithm but it cannot be applied to other approximation allocation algorithms. Also the mechanism is incentive compatible only when single-minded bidders are assumed[11].

The main problem in which VCG-based pricing is applied to approximation allocation of items is that there are the cases that: (1) the price for a won bid is rather higher than the bid price, and (2) the price for a won bid is less than zero, it means the bidder will win the items and also will obtain some money rather than paying for it[15]. In the situation of (1), it breaks individual rationality (i.e., the one will not pay a higher price than the placed bid when the one won the bundle of items). Also the situation of (2) is not preferable for both auctioneers and sellers.

## 2.4   Approximation for Multi-unit Combinatorial Auctions

In this section, we briefly describe the approximation allocation algorithm for multi-unit combinatorial auctions proposed in [5], as follows.

The inputs are *Alloc*, *L*, and *Stocks*. *L* is the bid list of an auction. *Stocks* is the list of the number of auctioned units for each distinguishable item type. *Alloc* is the initial greedy allocation of items for the bid list.

```
1: function LocalSearch(Alloc, L, Stocks)
2:    RemainBids:= L - Alloc;
3:    sortByLehmannC(RemainBids);
4:    for each b ∈ RemainBids
5:       RestStocks:=getRestStocks({b}, Stocks);
6:       AllocFromWinners:=greedyAlloc(RestStocks, Alloc);
7:       RestStocks:=
8:          getRestStocks(AllocFromWinners + {b}, RestStocks);
9:       AllocFromRest:=
10:         greedyAlloc(RestStocks, RemainBids − {b});
```

```
11:    NewAlloc:=
12:       {b} + AllocFromWinners + AllocFromRest;
13:    if price(Alloc) < price(NewAlloc) then
14:       return LocalSearch(NewAlloc,L,Stocks);
15:    end for each
16:    return Alloc
```

The function $sortByLehmannC(Bids)$ has an argument $Bids$. The function sorts the list of bids $Bids$ by descending order of Lehmann's weighted bid price. The result are directly stored (overwritten) to the argument $Bids$. The function $getRestStocks(Bids, Stocks)$ has two arguments : $Bids$ and $Stocks$. The function returns how many unit of items will remain after allocating the items in $Stocks$ to the list of bids $Bids$. The function $greedyAlloc(Stocks, Bids)$ has two arguments : $Stocks$ and $Bids$. The function allocates the items in $Stocks$ to the list of bids $Bids$ by using Lehmann's greedy allocation, and then the winner bids are returned as the return value. The function $price$ calculates the sum of bidding prices for bids specified in the argument.

The optimality of allocations got by Lehmann's algorithm (and the following hill-climbing) deeply depends on which value was set to the bid sorting criterion $c$. Again, in [11], Lehmann et al. argued that $c = 1/2$ is the best parameter for approximation when the norm of the worst case performance is considered. However, the optimal values for each auction are varied from 0 to 1 even if the number of items is constant. Therefore, an enhancement has been proposed for this kind of local search algorithms by using parallel searches for multiple sorting criterion $c$[6]. Although the proposed enhancement is primarily designed for single-unit combinatorial auctions, this approach can be applied to the above mentioned approximation algorithm for multi-unit combinatorial auctions. In the algorithm, the value of $c$ for Lehmann's algorithm is selected from a predefined list. It is reasonable to select $c$ from neighbors of $1/2$, namely, $C = \{0.0, 0.1, \ldots, 1.0\}$. The results are aggregated and the best one (i.e., that has the highest revenue) is selected as the final result.

To realize a pricing mechanism that receives little effect from the winners bid prices, we use the following algorithm. Here, the function $transformToSWPM$ calculates the prices and associated updated winners as well, to keep a condition called *strong winner price monotonicity*[5]. The inputs are $Alloc$, $L$, and $Stocks$. $L$ is the bid list of an auction. $Stocks$ is the list of the number of auctioned units for each distinguishable item type. $Alloc$ is the initial allocation of items for the bid list that is obtained by the previously defined $LocalSearch$ function.

```
1:  function transformToSWPM(Alloc, L, Stocks)
2:    RemainBids:= L - Alloc;
3:    sortByLehmannC(RemainBids);
4:    clear(payment);
5:    for each b ∈ Alloc
6:       RestStocks:=getRestStocks(Alloc − {b}, Stocks);
```

7:     $AllocForB := greedyAlloc(RestStocks, RemainBids)$;

8:     $NewAlloc := Alloc\text{-}\{b\} + AllocForB$;

9:     **if** $price(Alloc) < price(NewAlloc)$ **then**

10:      **return** transformToSWPM$(NewAlloc,L,Stocks)$;

11:    **else** $payment_b = price(NewAlloc) - price(Alloc - \{b\})$

12:  **end for each**

13:  **return** $(Alloc, payment)$

The above algorithm computes the price to be paid for each winner bid. The payment price for a winner bid $b$ is denoted by $payment_b$, and it's value is obtained by $price(NewAlloc) - price(Alloc - \{b\})$. When the obtained payment price is higher than the bidding price of the winner bid, the algorithm discards the winner bid and place the items to $AllocForB$. To the end, the algorithm produces modified allocations $Alloc$ and their payment prices $payment$ that satisfies budget constraints for bidders.

For simplicity of description, the above algorithm is written with single-minded bidders assumption. To extend the algorithm without the assumption can be realized by just replacing $\{b\}$ with the all bids that come from the bidder of $\{b\}$.

## 3   Applying to Electric Power Allocation

In this section, we present how an electric power allocation problem can be transformed into *a sequence of* multi-unit combinatorial auctions[2].

### 3.1   The Allocation Model

First of all, we would start from a very simple case.

*Single power source, one time slot:*    Here we assume there is a single power source and allocate electric power consumption rights in a small time unit $t$. In this case, each bidder should place a bid that denotes the amount of necessary electric power and the possible highest price to be paid for it. For example, one can place a bid for the use of 50W in duration $t$ with 0.04 Euro. This case is identical to a multi-unit (single-item) auction. When there are multiple preferences for different amounts of necessary electric power, e.g., 50W with 0.04 Euro but when it is for 40W the price becomes 0.02 Euro, such two bids can be placed at once, but each of them should include a dummy virtual item $i_d$ in their bundle of items. Here, the dummy item $i_d$ would be assigned to each bidder and which stock is always one. Therefore, the bidder only wins each of them at once but does not win both of them. This case is a simple case of a multi-unit combinatorial auction.

*Single power source, multiple time slots:*    In some cases, we may need to use electricity continuously during a certain time period. For example, when

_____

[2] A preliminary idea has been presented in [9].

operating a cloth washing machine, it takes a certain time period for its operation but the power supply should not be stopped during the operation time. In such case, we can include multiple time slots in an auction. A right to use electricity during multiple slots will be actually allocated when its first timeslot is reached to the current. Then, the occupied electric power will be removed from the auction in the next time. Otherwise the auction has the tentative winners but they will not be the final winners and it will continue the auction to accept further bids for unallocated electricity. This is a multi-unit combinatorial auction and also partly behaves as an ascending auction[3]. In this paper, we call it a *Multi-Round* auction approach.

*Multiple power sources, single time slot:*    We can consider the difference of power sources in bidding. For example, let there are two power sources $p_a$ and $p_b$ at a time slot $t$. We can only place a bid for power source $p_a$ but not for $p_b$ when $p_a$ is the preferable power source(e.g., a solar power generator) but $p_b$ is not (e.g., a nuclear generator). Also we can place a bid for a mixture use of $p_a$ and $p_b$, e.g., 500W from $p_a$ and 50W from $p_b$, within a single combinatorial bid. This case is similar to a case in *single power source, multiple time slots* but it places for different power sources in a same time slot. Also one can place a set of combinations of such mixtures but at most only one mixture can be won, by using a dummy item which is described before.

*Multiple power sources, multiple time slots:*    This is the most complicated case and it can be an extension of both *Single power source, multiple time slots* case and *Multiple power sources, single time slot* case. For example, one can place a bid for a period from $t_1$ to $t_2$ with the use of 500W from power source $p_a$ and 20W from power source $p_b$. Also in such biddings, the actual power usage for each time slot can be varied rather than a simple combination of fixed values for each power sources.

Note that, in the above model, we do not consider how the obtained revenue should be distributed to the power suppliers. Also it is assumed that a power supplier has the responsibility to produce the certain power at the specified time slot when it is allocated to consumers. When the power source cannot supply sufficient power in the time slot, the power source should buy the power from sufficient power sources via another auction. Therefore if there does not exist enough power supply from sufficient power sources in the market at the moment the power may not be supplied.

## 3.2   Example

Here we will give some examples for our approach. Since an important issue in using sustainable power sources is their uncontorollability and uncertainty of power generation levels(Fig.2), we will show how this issue can be captured in and handled by our proposed allocation model.

Fig. 3 shows an example of the expected power generation levels at time slot from 10:00 to 12:00 in each 30 minutes. For example, in a time slot between

---

[3] An analysis about this type of auction has been presented in [4].

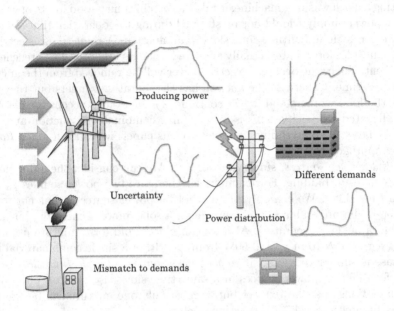

Producing power

Uncertainty

Mismatch to demands

Power distribution

Different demands

**Fig. 2.** Mismatches among Electricity Generation and Consumption Needs

10:00 and 10:30, we have 7 units of electric power supply. Since the level may depend on its time, the supply level is 1 unit greater than the slot between 10:30 and 11:00.

Fig. 4 shows an example of winner determination result based on a combinatorial biddings to the expected power supplies. Here, we can place a bid for a set of each 3 units at the slots from 10:00 to 12:00 (e.g., bid **d**). Of course a bid for single time slot can be placed (e.g., bid **a** and **c**). Here, in this case, when the first time slot reaches the current time, these units are allocated to the winners for the slot (i.e., bid **a** and **d**). Note that the bid **d** is for a bundle of multiple time slots, the units for other bundled time slots are also allocated to the bid **d** (Fig. 4:right).

Here, we consider what may happen when there is an update of expected power supply levels. Fig. 5 shows an example of such situation. Here, in Fig. 5(left), 1) there is a decrease of unit between 11:00 and 11:30, and 2) another bid (the bid **e**) appears. In this case, the bid **b** has no longer assigned to use any units but rather the bid **e** and another bid **f** obtained new allocations, since the total revenue of the auction is increased by doing so. Then, after reaching the time of the next slot (i.e., from 10:30 to 11:00), the units are allocated to winners of the slot as we described before (i.e., Fig. 5:right).

In this way, the rights to use electricity power supplies are allocated to winners of the *current* slot and their bundled units in other slots, repeatedly.

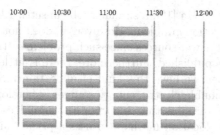

**Fig. 3.** Expected Power Generation Level in Each Time-Slot

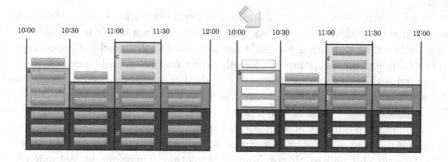

**Fig. 4.** Initial Bidding and Winner Determination

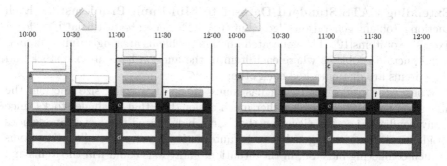

**Fig. 5.** Reallocation Due to Changes of Expected Supply Levels

## 4  Discussion

### 4.1  The Way of Performance Evaluation

Since there is no standard benchmark setting to evaluate electric power allocation performance that considers the consumers' preferences of power sources, we need to prepare a certain setting that reflects the important characteristics of the allocation problem that are discussed in this paper.

To our best knowledge, in [12], a similar problem setting has been introduced as a combinatorial auction problem. However, it does not consider such consumer's preferences of power sources since such problem setting was not realistic enough when [12] was published. Furthermore, there is little analysis about the change of our life when we have this kind of allocation mechanism and a rich amount of such sustainable electric energy sources. Therefore it is hard to prepare a set of realistic profiles that incorporates actual users' and producers' behaviors. Since our allocation mechanism uses a pricing mechanism that does not directly reflect the winners' bidding prices for their payments, we expect that we do not have to conduct an experiment with agents which dynamically learn the average market price in each time to adjust their behaviors, conducted in [17].

As a first step, it is meaningful to use a general evaluation dataset that somewhat reflects the characteristics, e.g., multi-unit problem which large amount of bids, rather than preparing a pseudo simulation of such a world. This is helpful to evaluate how an algorithm can handle a certain size of problems well.

For general evaluation of winner determination performance on combinatorial auction, LeytonBrown et al. proposed CATS benchmark testsuite[12].The CATS suite includes most of important ways to generate pseudo single-unit auction problems used on evaluations in the area[12]. However, although multi-unit auction is referred in [12], CATS suite does not include any concrete data generation algorithm for multi-unit combinatorial auction. Therefore, we extended the existing auction problem generation algorithm to support multi-unit auctions by the following way.

**Extending CATS Standard Dataset to Multi-unit Problems:**    Each auction problem generation algorithm in CATS generates artificial bids for a fixed size of items[12]. The generated auction problems are single-unit combinatorial auction problems where each item in the auction has only one stock and these items are distinguished each other.

When we consider each item has many stocks in a small size auction, the allocation problem could be rather much easier than that of single stocks since many conflicts (i.e., the situation that some bids placed to a set that includes an identical item) among bids can be automatically solved by allocating items to such conflicting bids. So, in the situation, many bids could win the items and only a limited number of bids might fail to win the items.

However, when there are a huge number of bids in a single-unit combinatorial auction, the problem could be complex enough even when we assume there are a small number of stocks for each item in the auction. Here, we extend the dataset produced by CATS workbench by adding number of stocks for each non-dummy item in an auction. We call this 'a number of stocks for each item' approach.

This representation is also useful for representing items that can be shared with a limited number of people. For example, when we represent a fact that a radio frequency band can be shared by three devices at a time, the stocks for the item (i.e., the number of shared users for the bandwidth) is set to 3 in the auction. Also this representation does not have to generate a large number of bids even when the number of stocks is large. Another representation could be based on a representation of indistinguishable relationships among items but this representation inevitably generates a large number of definitions for such relationships. Therefore, we use 'the number of stock for each item' approach here.

The actual preparations of datasets have been done as follows. We used the bid distributions (i.e., the way to generate bids for items) that are defined and usable for generating the auction problems with a specified number of bids. Here we choose 20,000 bids for each auction so we choose the bid distribution L2, L3, L4, L6, L7, arbitrary, matching, paths, regions, and scheduling[4]. We prepared 100 auction problems for each bid distribution for both the size of 20,000 bids in an auction. We used those settings to make the results comparable to other papers[7]. The names for bid distributions are borrowed from [12][5]. Here, to keep the meaning of data generation algorithms, we choose fixed values for those stocks (e.g., every item has 4 stocks). We chose a fixed value, 16 for these stocks[6].

Note that, as mentioned before, in multi-unit auction problems, some bids that could be treated as dominated bids(e.g., having a higher price of bid for the same bundle of items) in single-unit auction problems could be winners of the auction. Therefore, we did not eliminate such bids to generate the original single-unit auction problems by CATS.

**Compared Algorithms:**    In [5], we have compared the following search algorithms: greedyL(C=0.5) uses Lehmann's greedy allocation algorithm[11] with parameter ($c = 0.5$). MHC(c=0.5) and MHC-3 are the proposed multi-unit enabled algorithms extended from HC(c=0.5) and HC-3, respectively. Here, HC(c=0.5) uses a local search in which the initial allocation is Lehmann's allocation with $c = 0.5$ and conducts the hill-climbing search[6]. HC-3 uses the best results of the hill-climbing search with parameter ($0 \leq c \leq 1$ in 0.5 steps)[6],[7]. greedyO means a simple greedy allocation of the received bids by the input order. cplex is the result of CPLEX with the specified time limit.

**Comparison Criteria:**    Since it is really difficult to obtain the maximum revenue for an auction problem[12][11], we have compared algorithms with the values computed by average revenue ratio[7]. We use the same approach to evaluate performances of algorithms on single-unit auction problems.

Here, we use another approach that is based on the optimality ratio to the best one in the average on each bid distribution.

Let $A$ be a set of algorithms, $L$ be a dataset generated for this experiment, and $revenue_a(p)$ such that $a \in A$ be the revenue obtained by algorithm $a$ for a

---

[4] The reason why there are some missing number (e.g., L1, and L5,) is mainly the difficulty of generating the necessary number of bids by such bid distributions[12].

[5] For more details about each bid distribution, see [12].

[6] Actually we conducted our experiments in four fixed values, 2, 4, 16, and 256 for the number of stocks. Due to limited space of the paper, we only presented the results for 16 stocks. Further detailed analysis can be found in [5].

**Table 1.** Average Winner Determination Performance on Multi-Unit Auctions (20,000bids-256items,with dominated bids,stocks=16)

| | MHC-3-para-100ms | MHC-3-para-1000ms | greedyL(c=0.5) | greedyO | cplex-1000ms | cplex-3000ms |
|---|---|---|---|---|---|---|
| average | 0.9930 (100) | 0.9984 (1000) | 0.9570 (6.6) | 0.6745 (0.7) | 0.2245 (1050) | 0.4297 (2627) |

(each value in () is time in milliseconds)

problem $p$ such that $p \in L$, the average revenue ratio $ratioM_a(L)$ for algorithm $a \in A$ for dataset $L$ is defined as follows:

$$ratioM_a(L) = \frac{\sum_{p \in L} revenue_a(p)}{\max_{m \in A}(\sum_{p \in L} revenue_m(p))}$$

Here, we use $ratioM_a(L)$ for our comparison of algorithms on multi-unit auction problems. We also showed actual computation time for obtaining the approximation allocations.

**Evaluating Pricing Performance:**     In addition to above-mentioned comparisons, we compared the performance of the proposed pricing mechanism. Since the pricing mechanism itself may modify allocations, we compared the algorithms in $ratioM$, and execution time to complete allocations and pricing. In this paper, due to the limited space of the paper, we only show the comparison to evaluate pricing performance on greedyO, greedyL(c=0.5), and our approach(MHC-3-para-100ms). Since the value in CPLEX was very low in the setting, we omitted it in the results.

**Preliminary Experiment Environment:**     We implemented algorithms in a C program for the following experiments. The experiments were done with above implementations to examine the performance differences among algorithms. The programs were employed on a Mac with Mac OS X 10.4, a CoreDuo 2.0GHz CPU, and 2GBytes of memory.

### 4.2   Preliminary Analysis

Table 1 shows the allocation-only performance of each winner determination algorithm in $ratioM$[7]. Here, we can see the performance of MHC-3-para is clearly better than that in cplex within the same execution time. However, greedyL(c=0.5) is good enough in the ratio with very short execution time. Although the performance in ration of greedyO is not so high, its execution time is very fast.

Table 2 shows the performance $ratioM$ of approximate winner determination when the proposed pricing mechanism is applied for each approximate allocation obtained by the shown approximate winner determination algorithms. Although the actual execution time for the pricing mechanism deeply depends on the number of winners in each auction problem, the average of total execution time

---

[7] Further detailed analysis can be found in [5].

**Table 2.** Detailed Pricing Performance on Multi-Unit Auctions (20,000bids-256items,with dominated bids,stocks=16)

|  | MHC-3-para-100ms | greedyL(c=0.5) | greedyO |
|---|---|---|---|
| L2 | 1.0000 (157) | 0.9994 (57) | 0.6932 (6057) |
| L3 | 1.0000 (744) | 0.9988 (764) | 0.7064 (36503) |
| L4 | 1.0000 (414) | 0.9705 (23761) | 0.8664 (66774) |
| L6 | 1.0000 (292) | 0.9497 (7207) | 0.7380 (34904) |
| L7 | 1.0000 (475) | 0.9771 (364) | 0.7886 (1091) |
| arbitrary | 1.0000 (13273) | 0.9577 (4071) | 0.8883 (6483) |
| matching | 1.0000 (19633) | 0.9996 (22137) | 0.9718 (118207) |
| paths | 1.0000 (95337) | 0.9969 (84245) | 0.9889 (49906) |
| regions | 1.0000 (26031) | 0.9731 (14288) | 0.9461 (18883) |
| scheduling | 1.0000 (140) | 1.0000 (51) | 0.9663 (58) |
| average | 1.0000 (15650) | 0.9823 (15695) | 0.8554 (33886) |

(each value in () is time in milliseconds)

on MHC-3-para-100ms is rather faster than that on greedyO, and also it is slightly faster than that on greedyL(c=0.5). Furthermore, the performance *ratioM* of MHC-3-para-100ms is higher than the others. This shows that the combination of MHC-3-para-100ms and the proposed pricing mechanism can work better than other combinations on the experiment setting. When we apply our algorithm to a sustainable electric power auction, we may obtain 17 percent of energy gain compared to a simple fast-in fast-allocate mechanism(greedyO) and even about 2 percent better than sort-and-allocate approach(greedyL) although its average computation time is slightly short.

Note that, in this evaluation, we kept the size of auction problems rather small due to make the evaluation comparable to CPLEX. This is only for starting discussions and more sophisticated way of evaluation should be considered in the future research.

### 4.3    Issues Left

As we described before, in the proposed auction model, we do not consider how the obtained revenue should be distributed to the power suppliers. When we consider this issue, the problem becomes to *combinatorial exchange*[16]. In this paper we do not provide any idea to solve this issue.

Also in this model, it is assumed that a power supplier has the responsibility to produce the certain power at the specified time slot when it is allocated to consumers. This may not be realistic enough, for example, when a big accident happens (e.g., a bid disaster removes a large amount of solar power stations). In such cases, it would be very hard to buy a sufficient amount of electric power from the market so the allocations for the consumers would be discarded.

Since the auction used in the model can be seen as a combination of one-shot auction and ascending auction, it is difficult to present a strict theoretical analysis for the auction. It would be more complex than that of ordinary online auctions(i.e., typically they allocate only one item for each round but in the proposed model many items can be allocated at once).

Also this does not reflect any legal issues and moral and ethical issues. The model may enforce people who don't have enough money to have little opportunity to obtain electricity when the total power supply level is low. Also the model may produce the situation that a plant may blackout even when it would produce serious environmental damages. The model does not consider such social costs that should be paid by the society itself.

## 5    Conclusions

In this paper, we discussed about a preliminary idea and an analysis about a dynamic electric power auction when there are sustainable power sources and consumers have their preferences to use. We illustrated how such an auction can be formalized as a variant of multi-unit combinatorial auctions when we only consider the allocation of aggregated electricity. We discussed about a possible performance based on a standard evaluation dataset which rather does not consider actual power use scenarios. Also we discussed the potential advantages and issues left in the presented analysis. Further analysis and implementations will be presented in future work.

**Acknowledgements.** The work was partly supported by Japan Cabinet Founding Program for NEXT Generation World-Leading Researchers(NEXT Program), and Grants-in-Aid for Young Scientists(B) 22700142.

## References

1. Carrasco, J.M., Bialasiewicz, J.T., Guisado, R.C.P., Leon, J.I.: Power-electronic systems for the grid integration of renewable energy sources: A survey. IEEE Trans. Industrial Electronics 53(4), 1002–1016 (2006)
2. Cramton, P., Shoham, Y., Steinberg, R.: Combinatorial Auctions. The MIT Press (2006)
3. Fukuta, N., Ito, T.: Periodical resource allocation using approximated combinatorial auctions. In: Proc. of The 2007 WIC/IEEE/ACM International Conference on Intelligent Agent Technology (IAT 2007), pp. 434–441 (2007)
4. Fukuta, N., Ito, T.: Approximated winner determination for a series of combinatorial auctions. In: Proc. of 1st International Conference on Agents and Artificial Intelligence (ICAART 2009), pp. 400–407 (2009)
5. Fukuta, N.: Toward a VCG-like approximate mechanism for large-scale multi-unit combinatorial auctions. In: Proc. IEEE/ACM/WIC International Conference on Intelligent Agent Technology (IAT 2011), pp. 317–322 (2011)
6. Fukuta, N., Ito, T.: Towards better approximation of winner determination for combinatorial auctions with large number of bids. In: Proc. of The 2006 WIC/IEEE/ACM International Conference on Intelligent Agent Technology (IAT 2006), pp. 618–621 (2006)

7. Fukuta, N., Ito, T.: Fine-grained efficient resource allocation using approximated combinatorial auctions–a parallel greedy winner approximation for large-scale problems. Web Intelligence and Agent Systems: An International Journal 7(1), 43–63 (2009)
8. Fukuta, N., Ito, T.: An experimental analysis of biased parallel greedy approximation for combinatorial auctions. International Journal of Intelligent Information and Database Systems 4(5), 487–508 (2010)
9. Fukuta, N., Ito, T.: Toward combinatorial auction-based better electric power allocation on sustainable electric power systems. In: Proc. International Workshop on Sustainable Enterprise Software (SES 2011), pp. 392–399 (2011)
10. Hoos, H.H., Boutilier, C.: Solving combinatorial auctions using stochastic local search. In: Proc. of the 17th National Conference on Artificial Intelligence (AAAI 2000), pp. 22–29 (2000)
11. Lehmann, D., O'Callaghan, L.I., Shoham, Y.: Truth revelation in rapid, approximately efficient combinatorial auctions. Journal of the ACM 49, 577–602 (2002)
12. Leyton-Brown, K., Pearson, M., Shoham, Y.: Towards a universal test suite for combinatorial auction algorithms. In: Proc. of ACM Conference on Electronic Commerce (EC 2000), pp. 66–76 (2000)
13. MacKay, J.: Sustainable Energy - Without Hot Air, UIT Cambridge (2009)
14. McMillan, J.: Selling spectrum rights. The Journal of Economic Perspectives (1994)
15. Nisan, N., Ronen, A.: Computationally feasible VCG mechanisms. In: Proc. of ACM Conference on Electronic Commerce, pp. 242–252 (2000), citeseer.ist.psu.edu/nisan00computationally.html
16. Parkes, D.C., Cavallo, R., Elprin, N., Juda, A., Lahaie, S., Lubin, B., Michael, L., Shneidman, J., Sultan, H.: Ice: An iterative combinatorial exchange. In: The Proc. 6th ACM Conf. on Electronic Commerce (EC 2005) (2005)
17. Ramchurn, S.D., Vytelingum, P., Rogers, A., Jennings, N.: Agent-based control for decentralized demand side management in the smart grid. In: Proc. 10th International Conference on Autonomous Agents and Multiagent Systems (AAMAS 2011), pp. 5–12 (2011)
18. Sandholm, T., Suri, S., Gilpin, A., Levine, D.: Cabob: A fast optimal algorithm for winner determination in combinatorial auctions. Management Science 51(3), 374–390 (2005)
19. Zurel, E., Nisan, N.: An efficient approximate allocation algorithm for combinatorial auctions. In: Proc. of the Third ACM Conference on Electronic Commerce (EC 2001), pp. 125–136 (2001)

# A Co-dependent Value-Based Mechanism for the Internet Advertisement Auction

Satoshi Takahashi[1], Tokuro Matsuo[2], Takayuki Ito[3], and Roger Y. Lee[4]

[1] Graduate School of Systems and Information Engineering,
University of Tsukuba, Japan
takahashi2007@e-activity.org
[2] Graduate School of Science and Engineering,
Yamagata University, Japan
matsuo@yz.yamagata-u.ac.jp
[3] Graduate School of Engineering,
Nagoya Institute of Technology, Japan
ito.takayuki@nitech.ac.jp
[4] Software Engineering & Information Tech. Institute,
Central Michigan University, USA
roger.yim.lee@cmich.edu

**Abstract.** Advertisements on the webpage provide good opportunity to get new customers. In recent years, a lot of webpages providing a search service have advertisements, which are related with searched word by user. A basic structure of the Internet advertisement is that the service providers decide order of placement of many advertisements and advertising fees by auctions when advertisers offer their promotions. Generalized Second Price Auction (GSP) mechanism is most efficient auction mechanism of the advertisement auction. Some searching companies, such as Google and Yahoo, employ GSP mechanism basically. There are many researches on GSP in order to analyze and clarify its feature and advantages. However, these researches assume that traded advertisements are mutually independent. It means that each advertisement does not influence other advertisements. Also these researches do not consider a value of advertisement, which means some criterions of a name value of a company, an effectiveness and an importance, that is dependently each other. This paper proposes a new advertisement auction mechanism based on GSP with considering the co-dependent value of advertisement. We analyze the auctioneer's profit in comparison between normal GSP, normal VCG (Vickrey-Clarke-Groves Mechanism) and our proposed mechanism.

## 1 Introduction

In this paper, we give an analysis of agent-based advertisement auction, which is displayed on a webpage. Internet advertisement auction is one of important income source for some search engines such as Yahoo! and Google[1][2]. Some searching companies have some advertising spaces on own webpages and allocates it for some advertisers based on an advertising fee. As same as items trading in the Internet auctions, a displayed advertisement on web page is also based on the auction, called the Internet

S. Cranefield and I. Song (Eds.): PRIMA 2011 Workshops, LNAI 7580, pp. 64–77, 2012.
© Springer-Verlag Berlin Heidelberg 2012

advertisement auction. When users search for some words on the search engine, an advertisement related with the searched keywords is displayed with result of search[3]. The order of advertisements to be displayed is determined based on bid value in an auction. Advertisers can set up the interval and period to display the advertisement as a time slot. The advertising fee is determined based on the Generalized Second Price Auction, which is known higher revenues than the Generalized Vickrey Auction[4]. A winner in the auction gets a space to display their advertisement and the web page owner allocates time and position in the web page to show the advertisement. There are a lot of contributions about GSP(Generalized Second Price Auction) researches in electronic commerce research. In this auction, bidding and winner determination are conducted multiple time. Advertiser advertiser can change his/her bid value because the auction is continued with repetition. When advertisers try to bid in an auction, they bid on their strategy. However, GSP has an envy free equilibrium and webpage owner providing advertisement space can get larger benefit compared with VCG (Vickrey-Clark-Groves) Mechanism.

Generally, possibility of click is high order of display. This means that the advertisement fee of top-displayed advertisement is more expensive than lower advertisements. Google earned about 5.2 million USD by this advertisement system in 2008.

In previous research, the value of advertisement is assumed as independent with each other. Otherwise, some of their researches do not refer the value of the advertisement. However, each advertisement has a certain value for users. It means some criterions of a name value of a company, an effectiveness, an importance and an attribution, that is dependently each other. When same or similar item is soled in two e-commerce sites, the price on the advertisement is different from another one. If a buyer considers the price is important attribute to choose item, the advertisement selling items at low price has more value for the buyer. For example, a shop $A$ gives an advertisement to sell an item for $100. When a shop $B$ gives the advertisement to sell the same item for a shop $80, its value of the advertisement is higher than shop $A$'s value if the condition of item and other situations between shop $A$ and $B$. In this paper, we focus on such situation and simulate the revenue of advertisers. Also, we analyze a result of simulation of Internet advertisement auction with relationship between value of each advertisement. After the simulation, we reformulate our proposed model and mechanism based on the preliminary simulation. Concretely, we discuss about dynamical environment. It is more realistic situation of the advertisement market on the Internet.

The rest of this paper consists of the following four parts. In Section 2, we show preliminaries on several terms and concepts of auctions. In Section 3, we propose our value-based GSP and describe a preliminary experiment in some conditions. And we reformulate our proposed model and mechanism for applying a dynamic environment based on the preliminary simulation. Also we discuss some applications of the proposed model, especially about the GrobalAd system. Finally, we present our concluding remarks and future work.

## 2   Preliminaries

In this section, we describe a generally advertisement auction model. Suppose that there are $n$ advertisers and $k$ slots. A slot is a place of advertisement on a webpage. Let $c_i$

be a click-through-count (CTC) of the advertisement placed on the slot $i$. CTC is the number of clicks of the advertisement per an unit time. We assume following rule for each $c_i$:

$$c_{i-1} \geq c_i, \text{ for } 2 \leq i \leq k.$$

This rule means that CTC of the slot $i$ is lower than the slot $i-1$ for $2 \leq i \leq k$.

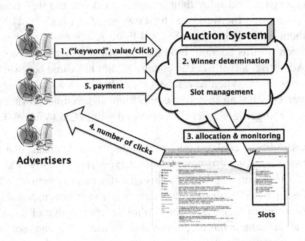

**Fig. 1.** Scheme of general Internet advertisement system

When an advertiser $j$ bids a pair of a keyword and value per click to use a slot as {"keyword", $b_j$}, a payment of the advertiser, who was allocated a slot $i$, is defined by $b_j \cdot c_i$. Figure 1 shows the generally advertisement auction model. In this model, there exists an advertisement auction system which decides some winners of the auction and management of slots. First of all, each advertiser bids some pairs of a keyword and value per click for advertisement slot to the auction system. After that, the auction system decides some winners of the auction and allocates the advertisements to the slots based on the bidding values. Also the auction system announces CTC to the winners, and the winner pays decided payment to the auction system.

The auction system employs some auction mechanisms for a winner determination. The auction mechanism is a rule of allocation and decision of payment. Generally, the auction mechanism describes the auction system. We introduce some typical auction mechanisms for the Internet advertisement auction. We assume every following auction satisfies Nash equilibrium. The Nash equilibrium shows that a strategy $S_A^\star$ is a best strategy for agent $A$ if every agent without agent $A$ chooses an optimal strategy $S^\star$.

**Vickrey auction mechanism.** Vickrey auction is an auction protocol which deals single item as same as second price sealed bid auction[4]. In this protocol, every advertiser bids own value for the auction system, which their bids do not be opened. A winner of the auction is the highest valued bidder, and he/she pays a second highest value of the auction. The Vickrey auction has week dominant strategy in which every advertiser bids own truth value. It is well known that the English and Dutch auction has also the same week dominant strategy[5].

**Vickrey-Clark-Groves (VCG) mechanism.** VCG mechanism is generalized from Vickrey auction, which has dominant strategy as truthful bidding[8]. Each advertiser $j$ bids own value per click for auctioneer. The auction system allocates a slot for the advertiser by descending order of bids. Suppose $\tilde{A}$ is a set of winners of the auction and $\tilde{A}^{-j}$ is a set of winners of the auction which eliminates the advertiser $j$, we define a payment per click $p_j$ of the winner as follows,

$$p_j = \sum_{k \in \tilde{A}^{-j}} b_k - \sum_{k \in \tilde{A}} b_k - b_j.$$

VCG mechanism satisfies incentive compatibility and Pareto efficiency under every bidders have the quasi linear utility functions. The Incentive compatibility (Strategyproofness) means that each advertiser choice an optimal strategy without influence of other advertisers. The Pareto efficiency means a total utilities of each advertiser and the auction system[4].

We show an example, suppose that there are two slots and three advertisers. Advertiser 1, 2 and 3 bids $300, $200 and $100 per click, respectively. In this case, the auction system allocates slot 1 and 2 to advertiser 1 and 2, and advertiser 1 and 2 pays $100 and $100 per click, respectively. Also, the auction system's gain is ($100 + $100) = $200.

**GFP (Generalized First Price Auction) mechanism.** This protocol is nearly single item first price auction, that is an advertiser who is a winner of the auction pays own value. The GFP protocol has dominant strategy for each advertiser. This protocol gives a highest utility for an advertiser when bids a lowest value he/she is able to win[5] . We consider an auction of one slot and two advertiser. If advertiser 1 and 2 bids $300 and $200, respectively, then the advertiser 1 get the slot. However, if the advertiser 1 bids $201, then also the winner. Therefore, GFP protocol has an incentive that every advertiser try to decrease own value. This means that the more increasing a number of advertisers, the more decreasing the auction system's gain.

**GSP (Generalized Second Price Auction) protocol.** GSP protocol is an auction protocol which is natural extended form second price auction[9]. The auction system sorts all bided values by descending order, and allocates slot $i$ to $i$-th highest valued advertiser for all slots. The advertiser who is allocated slot $i$ pays $b_{i+1}$ per click for the auction system.

It is known that GSP protocol does not satisfies incentive compatibility[10]. Therefore, the truthful bidding is not dominant strategy in GSP. On the other hands, GSP converges on Locally Envy Free equilibrium[6]. The auction is Locally Envy Free equilibrium, if an advertiser who gets a slot $i$ does not increase own utility neither getting a slot $i - 1$ nor getting a slot $i + 1$[11]. Hence, the slot $i$ is an optimal position which maximizes the advertisers' utility.

We consider the same example in VCG. Suppose that there are three advertisers and two slots, and advertiser 1, 2 and 3 bids $300, $200 and $100 per click. In this case, the advertiser 1 and 2 gets the slot 1 and 2, and pays $200 and $100 per click, respectively. The gain of auction system is $200 + $100 = $300. Therefore, the GSP protocol is better than VCG mechanism in the advertisement auction, since the auction systme gains $200 on the VCG mechanism. Note that if there is one slot, then the result of auction is the same on both GSP protocol and VCG mechanism.

Their mechanisms are employed not only the advertisement auction, but also the general Internet auction. Next we discuss an auction system of the Google Adwords.

## 2.1  Google Adwords

Google Adwords is an auction protocol similar to GSP protocol. Google Adwords employs CTR (Click-Through-Rate) and QS (Quality-Score). CTR is a ratio of click denoted by

$$CTR = \frac{\text{Click-through-count of an advertisement}}{\text{Number of page view of an advertisement}}$$

Quality score is decided by Google from CTR and relationship between text of the advertisement and searching keyword. Also, Google sets a minimum bidding value. An allocation of slots are based on descending order of multiplying the value by quality score, called *evaluation score*. It means that if high quality score has a possible to get a good position of slot by cheap payment. Google requires all advertisements positioned on upper slots must have a certain quality score level. Let $q$ be a quality score of an advertiser allocated on a slot $i$, and $b_i$ ($b_1 > b_2 > \cdots > b_i > \cdots > b_k$) be a evaluation score. A payment $p$ per click is denoted by

$$p = \frac{b_{i+1}}{q} + 1$$

It is known that CTR is proportional to order of slots. N. Brooks[7] say that there is a strong correlation between CTR and order of slots. The report also shows the ratios of CTR when a first ordered CTR is 100%. in this result, a second ordered is 77.4%, and third is 66.6%. However, Google suggests there is an exception. For example, some famous companies positioned lower slots has larger CTR than some upper positioned companies, since the famous companies get many click-through-counts even lower position.

On the other hand, Sponsored search which is derived by Yahoo! Search Marketing has technique similar to Google Adwords, but, there is a difference that order of slots is descending order of only bidding value.

We consider the same example in VCG. Suppose that there are three advertisers and two slots, and advertiser 1, 2 and 3 bids $300, $200 and $100 per click. Also advertiser 1, 2 and 3's quality score is 2, 1.5 and 1, respectively. In this case, the evaluate scores are 600, 300 and 100, respectively. The advertiser 1 and 2 gets the slot 1 and 2, and pays $300/2 = $150 and $100/1.5 = $66 per click. The gain of auctioneer is $150 + $66 = $216.

## 2.2  Our Advertisement Auction Model

Above mechanisms do not consider some value aside from advertising fee. It means a criterion of name value, effectiveness and importance for users. This criterion is not independent with each other, since users compare two or more advertisements for increasing them utilities. Thus each advertisement has a co-dependent value and it is expressed by linear to be evaluated.

Let $Ad$ $(|Ad| \leq k)$ be a set of advertisements which are now placed on the site, $Co(j) \subseteq \{1, ..., n\} \cap Ad$ be a set of co-dependent advertisements with advertisement $j$. When a value of company $j$'s advertisement changes $A_{after}^{j}$ from $A_{before}^{j}$, co-dependent value of other advertisement $\ell$ with company $j$ is shown $B_{before}^{\ell}$ and $B_{after}^{\ell}$. $B_{before}^{\ell}$ is changed a value effected by all advertisement in $Co(\ell)$ to $B_{after}^{\ell}$. That is

$$B_{after}^{\ell} = B_{before}^{\ell} + \alpha \sum_{j \in Co(\ell)} (A_{after}^{j} - A_{before}^{j}) \tag{1}$$

The condition of the above equation is given as $0 \leq \alpha \leq 1$. $\alpha = 0$ shows independent with each advertisement. Quality score in the GSP auction protocol used in Google Adwords is placed a value in which we have defined above definition in the simulation. Figure 2 is an example of the model of our proposed mechanism. When a user clicks the link of the advertisement, its value is increased. Relatively, other advertisement's value becomes going down. When low-ranked advertisement is clicked by users, the advertisement is regarded as valuable comparing with high-ranked advertisement. In the Figure 2, we assume all of advertisers participate to bid for the first time. After bidding, the winners are determined be the auction. Then, each advertisement is displayed at the website as (A). Users click the advantages and the value of each advertisement changes based on number of click as (B). After one period passes, advertisers bid at second round auction to keep their advertisement in the website. We also assume all advertiser bid same price comparing with first round auction. The order of advertisement is changed based on both bid price and advertisement's value. In this case, although advertisement 1's value decreased in (B), position of advertisement 1 is kept at top because bid price is very high as (C). Because advertisement 4's value is quite high in (B), the rank of advertisement in (C) becomes second although bid price is the lowest in other three advertisers.

Next, we show some preliminary experiments for evaluation of our proposed model, and for finding new conditions or characteristics.

# 3 Preliminary Experiment

## 3.1 Condition

We set 3-10 slots to be put advertisements and 10-50 advertisers (companies to join in the auction) who bid to get a space for their advertisement. The lowest bid price in the auction is set $10 and advertiser's bid value is defined a uniform distribution between $10 and $100. Initial value of each advertisement is defined on a uniform distribution between 0.2 and 2.2. Number of clicking by end-user is assumed on a uniform distribution between 1 and 100 in a time slot.

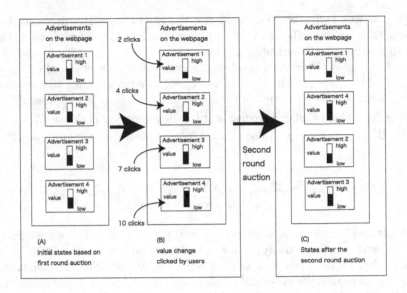

**Fig. 2.** Concept of the proposed mechanism

## 3.2 Procedure of Trade

We now simulate our proposing mechanism by using following procedure. The procedure gives in above condition.

1. Decide a number of slots for advertisements.
2. Decide a number of clicks for each slot in a period.
3. Decide each advertiser's bid value and advertisement value.
4. Allocate each slot in descending order according to a valuation that is multiplied by a bid price and a value of advertisement.
5. Calculate each advertiser's payment and benefit.
6. Change a value of advertisement of a certain advertiser.
7. Compute a new value of advertisement based on equation (1).
8. Conduct step 4) and 5) based on the new value of advertisement and bid price.

We run this procedure at 100 thousands times.

## 3.3 Results

Table 1 shows result of simulation in which value of advertisement is changed. There are 20 advertiser advertisers and value of a certain advertisement is reduced and it effects other values of advertisement. When number of slot is changed from 4 to 10 and a value of one advertisement is reduced, 54,000 auctions make whole profit in the market increase in 100,000 trial. Average of the increased profit is $21.38. We discuss result of simulation from Table 1.

**Table 1.** A value of one advertisement is reduced

| Number of slot | Increase (%) | Decrease (%) | Average of increased /decreased profit |
|---|---|---|---|
| 4 | 54.1 | 45.9 | $22.38 |
| 6 | 55.3 | 44.7 | $25.92 |
| 8 | 55.7 | 44.3 | $27.56 |
| 10 | 56.3 | 43.7 | $30.22 |

1. Averages of profit is normally increased and the profit increases when number of slots increases.
2. Possibility of profit increase is increased when number of slot increases.

This feature is apparent because the curve in Table 1 is monotonic increase.

As same as the above, Table 2 shows the case where 20 advertisers join in the auction and value of one advertiser's advertisement is increased. The number of slot is changed from 4 to 10 in each trial. We discuss result of simulation from Table 2.

**Table 2.** A value of one advertisement is increased

| Number of slot | Increase (%) | Decrease (%) | Average of increased /decreased profit |
|---|---|---|---|
| 4 | 43.8 | 56.2 | -$32.85 |
| 6 | 43.0 | 57.0 | -$36.63 |
| 8 | 42.2 | 57.8 | -$38.81 |
| 10 | 42.0 | 58.0 | -$40.31 |

1. Averages of profit is normally decreased and the profit decreases when number of slots increases.
2. Possibility of profit increase is decreased when number of slot increases.

This feature is also apparent because the curve in Table 1 is monotonic decrease.

Table 3 is a result where number of slot is fixed as 5 and one advertiser changes value of his/her advertisement. The number of advertiser is changed 10 to 50 in each trial. Rate of increase/decrease of value of advertisement is assumed by uniform distribution. The result shows a comparison of profits between non-affective and affective.

1. Averages of profit is normally decreased and the profit decreases when number of slots increases.
2. Possibility of profit increase is decreased when number of slot increases.

Average of profit is negative because possibility that the profit decreases is large. From above simulation and analysis, we find out the following features. First, total profit of webpage owner reduces when each advertisement has co-dependence between its value. Second, when the size of auction becomes large, average of profit is decreased.

**Table 3.** Number of slot is fixed as 5

| Number of advertisers | Increase (%) | Decrease (%) | Average of increased /decreased profit |
|---|---|---|---|
| 10 | 49.8 | 50.2 | -$2.81 |
| 20 | 49.1 | 50.9 | -$4.87 |
| 30 | 48.7 | 51.3 | -$5.17 |
| 40 | 48.3 | 51.7 | -$6.27 |
| 50 | 48.1 | 51.9 | -$6.85 |

### 3.4 Comparison to VCG

Table 4 shows the result of simulation when the number of advertisers is 20 and number of slots are changed from 4 to 10 in each trial. When number of advertiser increases, our proposed GSP mechanism makes large profit comparing with general VCG mechanism.

**Table 4.** A value of one advertisement is increased

| Number of slot | Increase (%) | Decrease (%) |
|---|---|---|
| 4 | 80.3 | 19.7 |
| 6 | 83.6 | 16.4 |
| 8 | 83.7 | 16.3 |
| 10 | 83.8 | 16.2 |

Table 5 shows the result of simulation when the number of slot is fixed as 5 in comparison between our proposed GSP and general VCG mechanism. Our proposed GSP makes larger profit compared with normal VCG with monotonic increase when the number of advertisers increases. When number of advertisers is not many, the increase rate is high. After number of advertisers is 30, increase rate becomes less and it seems to become convergence.

**Table 5.** Number of slot is fixed as 5

| Number of advertisers | Increase (%) | Decrease (%) |
|---|---|---|
| 5 | 51.6 | 48.4 |
| 10 | 62.3 | 37.7 |
| 20 | 82.9 | 17.1 |
| 30 | 89.5 | 10.5 |
| 40 | 92.8 | 7.2 |
| 50 | 94.5 | 5.5 |

To analyze more special case, we try to run a simulation when the number of slots are fixed as 3. We find out the following two features from the simulation. First, when number of advertiser increases, our GSP provides larger profit than VCG. Second, rate of increase becomes small when number of advertisers decreases.

## 4   Discussion

The preliminary experiment is static environment, however, the real is dynamic environment. The co-dependent evaluation, which is in our proposed model, should be decided dynamically. Figure 3 shows an image of dynamic changing of co-dependent values. In this figure, there are two advertisements, they influence each other. In dynamic environment, there is a deadline of co-dependent value decision. This deadline shows a time in which a final co-dependent value is decided. White circle and gray circle shows two advertisements' co-dependent value. In this figure, their initial states are fixed on time 0. When the white circle is going down, then this phenomenon influence the gray circle. Each co-dependent value iterates this phenomena until deadline. This image also shows in left part of figure 3.

In the dynamic environment, there are many advertisements which influence each other. Hence we should reformulate our proposed model and create efficient mechanism for a dynamic environment.

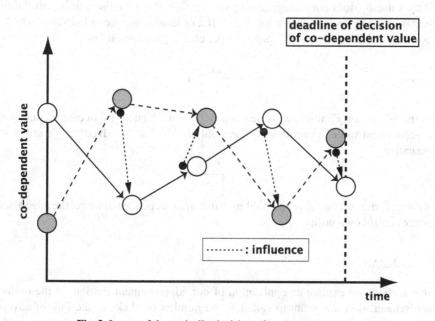

**Fig. 3.** Image of dynamically decision of co-dependent value

### 4.1   Reformulation

In this section, we reformulate our proposed model and an auction mechanism used by the model. Now we redefine some terms and formulas.

We assume that every advertisers has the quasi linear utility function. Suppose that there are $n$ advertisers and $k$ slots in the advertisement auction. Let $Ad$ ($|Ad| \leq k$) be a set of advertisements which are now placed on the site and $Co(j) \subseteq Ad$ be a set of co-dependent advertisements with advertisement $j$. Also let $C_j^t$ be a co-dependent value of $j$ at time $t$. $C_j^t$ is computed by the following:

$$C_j^t = C_j^{t-1} + \sum_{k \in Co(j)} \beta_k^t (C_k^t - C_k^{t-1}), \qquad (2)$$

where $\beta^t$ is a condition parameter. Also $C_j^t$'s range is $(0, 1]$. We define $\beta^t$ as a function on a co-dependent vector $\boldsymbol{C}^{t-1}$. Hence,

$$\beta_j^t := \beta_j^{t-1} + f(\boldsymbol{C}^{t-1}).$$

The auction system is able to compute the formulation 2 by using a simultaneous equation.

Next we reformulate an auction mechanism for the dynamic auction model. The auction system allocates each slot by descending order of a function of pair of the co-dependent value and advertiser's bids $g_j(C_j^t, b_j)$. Note that since an advertiser $j$'s bidding value $b_j$ does not change among the auction, the advertisement's position of slots is decided by only co-dependent value. If a ordered sequence of bid value is $b_1 > b_2 > \cdots > b_j > b_{j+1} > \cdots b_n$, a payment per click $p_j^t$ is denoted by

$$p_j^t = \frac{b_{j+1}}{C_j^t} + 1.$$

Also the advertiser $j$'s utility$u_j$ is denoted by$p_j^t - b_j$. Hence, we decide a condition of co-dependent value. The following inequality holds that the advertiser $j$'s utility is nonnegative.

$$C_j^t \leq \frac{b_{j+1}}{b_j - 1}.$$

However, co-dependent value and bidding value are independent. Hence, the advertiser does not control own utility.

## 4.2    GlobalAd

In this section, we explain an application of our advertisement auction. In the online advertisement, it is important to calculate the number of clicks of the link of advertisement shown on the webpage. The number of successful trade after clicking an advertisement is also sometimes considered to know the quality of the advertisement. On the other hands, actual newspapers are not clicked by the subscribers, and business providers (who apply to publish their advertisement) may know the reputation of their advertisement from trading history using survey. Generally, because of the strong limitation of that, it is easier to make a formalization to determine winners in actual advertisement auction than the online advertisement auction, except for the constraints regarding space, multiple pages, position, and size.

There are some web-based advertisement application systems to be used in actual newspaper. None of them provide the procurement, winner-determination, and bidding mechanisms. The GlobalAd is a useful system to apply an advertisement that is used internationally. The GlobalAd is developed with a technology that will help a user to book its advertisement in any newspaper all over the world. Figure 4 shows the architecture of GlobalAd. First, a user will be able to select its preferences viz. its country, state, city, newspaper and date on which it wants to publish its advertisement in the selected newspaper. Upon selected preferences like size of the advertisement and newspaper, a bill is generated. If the user agrees to the amount in the bill, it is asked to upload its material on the database. After uploading the material, the user has to make payment via its credit/debit card or its bank account over a secured payment gateway of the Paypal. On making payment, a receipt is generated for the user. Also, an email of user preferences is sent to the advertisement agency on making the payment. On the basis of the preferences and the material uploaded by the user on the database, the advertisement agency books the advertisement in the newspaper selected by the user in its preferences. On the date selected by the user in its preferences, it can view the copy of the published advertisement in the newspaper by clicking a link on the Global Ad website. In this way, the Global Ad website will help a user book its advertisement in any newspaper of its choice all the world.

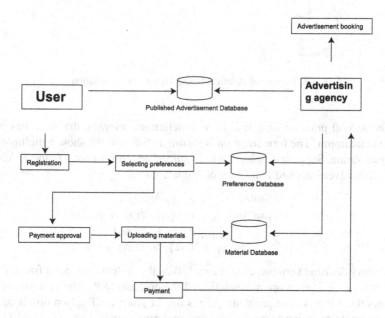

**Fig. 4.** System Architecture of GlobalAd

The GlobalAd currently provides the simple function explained above, however the combinations of users preferences are complicated; users have some preferences including advertisement's size, position, page, order, and cost. If users' some preferences are overlapped, it is rational to determine winners in the economics viewpoints. Namely, the auction type becomes applied multiple auctions or combinatorial auctions. Figure 5 shows the process using the auction-based winner determination in the GlobalAd.

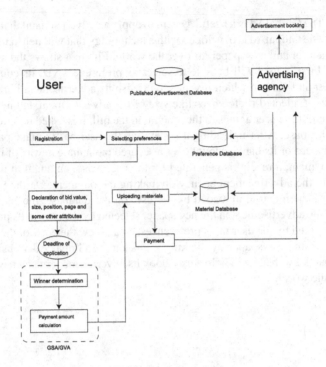

**Fig. 5.** Process of Auction-based Winner Determination

Using the second price auction, it is easy to determine winners, that becomes social surplus is maximum. The formalization is shown as follows. We show a multiple auction formalization. Suppose that $b_{ij}$ is a bid value of advertiser $i$ for a frame $j$. Also let $N$ be a set of advertisers and $F$ be a set of frames. Then,

$$(AP) \begin{vmatrix} \text{maximize } \sum_{i \in N} \sum_{j \in F} b_{ij} x_{ij} \\ \text{subject to } \sum_{j \in F} x_{ij} \leq 1, \forall i \in N \\ \sum_{i \in N} x_{ij} = 1, \forall j \in F \\ x_{ij} \in \{0, 1\}, \forall i \in N, j \in F \end{vmatrix}$$

$x_{ij}$ is a binary decision variable. If $x_{ij}$ takes 1, then the system allocates a frame $j$ to an advertiser $i$. Let $X^*$ be an optimal solution of the problem (AP). The optimal solution $X^*$ shows the winners. The problem (AP) is one of general allocation problems, it is easy to compute by using some integer programming solver such as CPLEX[12] or Gurobi[13]. There are some paid softwares, however, the problem (AP) is also able to solvable by using graph theoretical technique written by [14] and [15]. Our auction system employs a graph theory based algorithm.

## 5   Conclusion

This paper proposed a co-dependent value-based GSP mechanism in the Internet advertisement auctions. For analysis of the mechanism, we ran a preliminary simulation based on multi-agents. Our analysis showed that total profit changes in different auctions mechanism GSP, VCG, and our proposed mechanism. From the analysis, auctioneer changes the auction protocol based on his/her estimate profit. Our auction protocol had an advantage where the website provides more useful advertisement for users, because the order of allocation is based on both price and value. Also we reformulated our proposed model and mechanism for dynamic environment. The co-dependent value is changing dynamically among a few times. Our model showed this phenomena. And we introduced the GrobalAd system as an application of our advertisement mechanism. The GrobalAd system is already implemented as an advertisement allocation system for some paper medias. Also we discussed possible application of our advertisement auction mechanism for the system.

Our future work includes the analysis of profit and expected utility for agents in the mixed type of normal GSP, VCG, and our protocol. Also future work is evaluation of a dynamic model by some simulation.

# References

1. http://www.yahoo.com
2. http://www.google.com
3. Edelman, B., Ostrivsky, M., Schwarz, M.: Internet Advertising and the Generalized Second-Price Auction Selling of Dollars Worth of Keywords. The American Economic Review (2005)
4. Vickrey, W.: Couterspeculation, Auctions, and Competitive Sealed Tenders. Journal of Finance (1961)
5. Krishna, V.: Auction Theory. Academic Press (2002)
6. Edelman, B., Ostrovsky, M., Schwarz, M.: Internet Advertising and the Generalized Second Price Auction: Selling Billions of Dollars Worth of Keywords. American Economic Review 9(1), 242–259 (2007)
7. Brooks, N.: The Atlas Rank Report: How Search Engine Rank Impact Traffic. Insights, Atlas Institute Digital Marketing (2004)
8. Milgrom, P.: Putting Auction Theory to Work. Cambridge University Press (2004)
9. Varian, H.R.: Position auctions. International Journal of Industrial Organization (2005)
10. Abrams, Z., Schwarz, M.: Ad Auction Design and User Experience. In: Deng, X., Graham, F.C. (eds.) WINE 2007. LNCS, vol. 4858, pp. 529–534. Springer, Heidelberg (2007)
11. Guruswami, V., Hartline, J.D., Karlin, A.R., Kempe, D., Kenyon, C., McSherry, F.: On profit-maximizing envy-free pricing. In: Proceedings of the Sixteenth Annual ACM-SIAM Symposium on Discrete Algorithms, pp. 1164–1173 (2005)
12. http://www-01.ibm.com/software/integration/optimization/cplex-optimizer
13. http://www.gurobi.com/
14. Ahuja, R.K., Magnanti, T.L., Orlin, J.B.: Network Flows: Theory, Algorithms, and Applications. Prentice Hall (1993)
15. Korte, B.H., Vygen, J.: Combinatorial optimization: theory and algorithms. Springer (2008)

# Evaluation of Special Lanes as Incentive Policies for Promoting Electric Vehicles

Ryo Kanamori[1], Takayuki Morikawa[2], and Takayuki Ito[1]

[1] School of Techno-Business Administration, Nagoya Institute of Technology,
Gokiso-cho, Showa-ku, Nagoya, 466-8555, Japan
{kanamori.ryo,ito.takayuki}@nitech.ac.jp
[2] Department of Environmental Engineering and Architecture, Nagoya University,
Furo-cho, Chikusa-ku, Nagoya, 464-8603, Japan
morikawa@nagoya-u.jp

**Abstract.** In this study, we evaluate the effects of electric vehicle (EV) lanes in which only EV drivers enjoy the benefits of a reduction of travel time like the HOV lanes, and EV/Toll lanes whose charging system is similar to HOT lanes. The multi-class combined equilibrium model including a nested logit model to describe the traveler's behavior of each EV owners and non-owners is developed. The differences in service levels between EV drivers and non-EV drivers are not only a travel time under the special network for EV but also travel costs. If EV diffusion rate in the Nagoya metropolitan area is 10% and EV/Toll lanes are introduced, the incentive for owning EV is ensured, and the social surplus is improved than before the introduction of special lanes.

**Keywords:** Electric vehicle, EV and toll lane, Low-carbon society, Travel demand forecasting.

## 1    Introduction

For an early realization of transportation systems for the low-carbon society, some packaged transport policies involving P&R (park and ride) or road pricing have been introduced in several metropolitan areas. In addition, the low-emission vehicles such as PHV (plug-in hybrid vehicle) or EV (electric vehicle) are promoted actively owing to an innovation of car and battery technologies in recent years. The main promotions of these next generation cars in Japan are purchase supports by a subsidy or a tax reduction, but it is difficult to continue these measures by the lack of resources. Therefore it is important to examine the incentive to give convenience to driving an eco-car by introducing the special lanes or discounting the parking fees. Actually, it was reported that the number of EVs in Oslo, Norway has increased rapidly after giving these incentives.

Although there are a lot of researches of the influence on electricity demand by the diffusion of next generation vehicles [1], the study of incentives to own an EV is few. As a related research in special lanes, the evaluation of HOV (High-Occupancy

S. Cranefield and I. Song (Eds.): PRIMA 2011 Workshops, LNAI 7580, pp. 78–89, 2012.

Vehicle) lanes and HOT (High Occupancy vehicle and Toll) lanes seem to be included. HOT lanes are limited-access lanes reserved for buses and other high-occupancy vehicles (i.e. HOV lanes) but open to single occupant vehicles on payment of a toll. The policy that opening up the special lanes to low-emission cars is proposed in California and the impacts of incorporating hybrid vehicles into HOV lanes with a microscopic simulation are analyzed in [2]. But almost of related study of HOV and HOT lanes are concerned about the efficiency or equity [3] [4] [5] [6].

The objective of this paper is to evaluate the effects of special lanes as incentive policies for promoting EVs, especially we focus attention on EV lanes in which only EV drivers enjoy the benefits of a reduction of travel time like HOV lanes, and EV/Toll lanes whose charging system is similar to HOT lanes. The evaluation model is a multi-class combined equilibrium model including a nested logit model to describe the traveler's behavior of each EV owners and non-owners, and is applied to the network of a metropolitan area.

This paper is organized as follows. Section 2 describes the formulation of the multi-class combined equilibrium model and the estimation results of parameters in travel behavior model. Section 3 presents the influence of the penetration level of EV on urban traffic and environment improvement. The evaluation results of EV lanes and EV/Toll lanes are shown in Section 4. Finally, Section 5 summarizes this study findings and future works.

# 2    Multi-class Combined Equilibrium Model

## 2.1    Traveler Behavior

We assume that the traveler's behavior during a typical weekday morning peak period is expressed as the nested logit structure [7] shown in Fig. 1. This structure considers mode choice and route choice behavior.

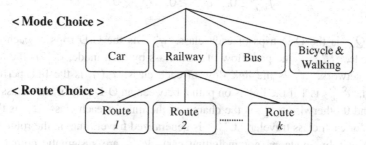

**Fig. 1.** Structure of the traveler choice process

## 2.2    Formulation of Multi-class Combined Equilibrium Model

The travel time on each link in the road network is expressed as the link performance function (i.e. the BPR function). Link travel time varies according to the link flow and the path flow, which is the result of traveler behavior. At the same time, the generalized travel time in the behavioral model varies according to the link travel time. Thus, we need to seek an equilibrium state between demand and supply. This stochastic user equilibrium state can be obtained by solving the following equivalent convex minimization problem—the Multi-class Combined Equilibrium Model [8] [9].

$$
\min. Z = \sum_a \int_0^{x_a} t_a(\omega) d\omega + \sum_{i,a} x_a^i \, p_a^i / \tau^i
$$

$$
+ \sum_{i,rs,m,k} \frac{1}{\theta_1^{i,m}} f_{m,k}^{i,rs} \ln(f_{m,k}^{i,rs} / q_m^{i,rs}) + \sum_{i,rs,m',k} f_{m',k}^{i,rs} \, C_{m',k}^{i,rs} \tag{1a}
$$

$$
+ \sum_{i,rs,m} \frac{1}{\theta_2^i} q_m^{i,rs} \ln(q_m^{i,rs} / Q_{rs}^i) + \sum_{i,rs,m} q_m^{i,rs} V_m^{i,rs}
$$

subject to

$$
x_a = \sum_{i,rs,k,a} f_{m,k}^{i,rs} \cdot \delta_{a,k}^{i,rs}, \qquad \forall a \tag{1b}
$$

$$
\sum_i x_a^i = x_a, \qquad \forall a \tag{1c}
$$

$$
\sum_k f_{m,k}^{i,rs} = q_m^{i,rs}, \qquad \forall i, rs, m \tag{1d}
$$

$$
\sum_m q_m^{i,rs} = Q_{rs}^i, \qquad \forall i, rs \tag{1e}
$$

$$
f_{m,k}^{i,rs} \ge 0, \quad q_m^{i,rs} \ge 0, \quad Q_{rs}^i \ge 0 \tag{1f}
$$

where $Q_{rs}^i$ is the O-D trips of each class, $q_m^{i,rs}$ is the O-D trips of each class by each mode, $f_{m,k}^{i,rs}$ is the path flow of each class by each mode, $x_a$ is the link flow in road network, $x_a^i$ is the link flow of each class, $t_a(\cdot)$ is the link performance function, $\delta_{a,k}^{i,rs}$ is 1 if the link is on path $k$ between an O-D pair of each class by each mode and 0 otherwise, $p_a^i$ is the charge on the link for each class, $\tau^i$ is the value of time for each class traveler, $C_{m',k}^{i,rs}$ is generalized travel time on the route between an O-D pair by mode $m'$(not including car), $V_m^{i,rs}$ are systematic components of mode choice, and $\theta_1^{i,m}$, $\theta_2^i$ are scale parameters.

It can be proved easily that this problem has a unique solution under these conditions (1b-1f). The Karush-Kuhn-Tucker condition for the problem leads to the aforementioned nested logit model with stochastic user equilibrium conditions.

$$f_{m,k}^{i,rs} = \frac{\exp[-\theta_1^{i,m} C_{m,k}^{i,rs}]}{\sum_k \exp[-\theta_1^{i,m} C_{m,k}^{i,rs}]} q_m^{i,rs} \tag{2a}$$

$$q_m^{i,rs} = \frac{\exp[-\theta_2^i (V_m^{i,rs} + S_m^{i,rs})]}{\sum_m \exp[-\theta_2^i (V_m^{i,rs} + S_m^{i,rs})]} Q_{rs}^i \tag{2b}$$

$$S_m^{i,rs} = -\frac{1}{\theta_1^{i,m}} \ln \sum_k \exp[-\theta_1^{i,m} C_{k,m}^{i,rs}] \tag{2c}$$

where $S_m^{i,rs}$ are inclusive values.

The partial linearization algorithm can be used to efficiently solve this problem. Even though the problem includes a path-flow entropy term, the model can be applied to large networks using entropy decomposition [10].

## 2.3    Estimation of Parameters in Nested Logit Model

In order to apply the multi-class combined equilibrium model to an actual situation, in this study the Nagoya Metropolitan Area in Japan, the parameters of nested logit model must be estimated. Traveler's behavior in this area was obtained from the 4th Nagoya Metropolitan Area Person Trip (PT) Survey conducted in 2001. The parameters are estimated based on this PT survey data by means of the maximum likelihood method [7].

Traffic conditions reported by the PT survey are assumed to correspond to the stochastic traffic equilibrium state. The average travel time during morning peak time in every road link is calculated from probe-vehicle data gathered in the Nagoya Metropolitan Area [11]. The level of service of railway and bus are calculated from the timetables respectively. Estimates of model parameters, as well as the analysis, are based on the PT minimum size zone, in which Nagoya City is divided into 258 zones with an average area of 1.25 km$^2$ (the total number of zones in the Nagoya Metropolitan Area is 515). We also consider intra-zonal O-D trips, the travel time is set to zero for car, bicycle and walking. The positive scale parameter for a car in route choice is set to 0.5 (1/minute). And the parameter of car travel time is set to -1.0 (minute).

The parameters of estimation results are shown in Table 1. The route choice model considers only car and railway travel because of the work involved in developing alternative route data. The parameters of the route choice model are common to two activities. Level of service, socio-economic characteristics and travel cost (i.e. gasoline and parking charges) are adopted as explanatory variables. All parameter has the expected sign and is statistically significant. The calculated value of time of car is 68.4 JPY per minute, and seems appropriate intuitively.

**Table 1.** Estimation results of route and mode choice

< Route Choice >

| | | Activity | |
|---|---|---|---|
| Mode | Variable | Commuting to Work | to School |
| Car | Scale parameter *1 | 0.50 | |
| | Travel time(min) *1 | -1.00 | |
| | Cost(100JPY) | -1.462 | |
| Railway | Scale parameter | 0.204 | |
| | In-vehicle time(min) | -0.377 | |
| | Out-of-vehicle time(min) | -0.899 | |
| | Cost(100JPY) | -4.475 | |
| | Access distance(km) | -6.963 | |
| | Egress distance(km) | -7.590 | |
| | Representative station *2 | 0.638 | |

< Mode Choice >

| | | Activity | |
|---|---|---|---|
| Mode | Variable | Commuting to Work | to School |
| | Scale parameter | 0.074 | 0.071 |
| Car | Gasoline & Parking charge(100JPY) *3 | -8.881 | -14.700 |
| | Driver's license | 3.082 | 2.533 |
| | Car Owner | 1.946 | - |
| | Male | 0.852 | - |
| Railway | Constant_inner Nagoya | 3.335 | 1.422 |
| | Constant_outer Nagoya | 2.863 | 1.262 |
| Bus | Constant | 4.028 | 1.253 |
| | In-vehicle time(min) | -0.672 | |
| | Out-of-vehicle time(min) | -0.569 | |
| | Cost(100JPY) | -4.475 | |
| | Access distance(km) | -13.466 | |
| | Egress distance(km) | -12.593 | |
| Biycle & | Constant_inner Nagoya | 6.014 | 4.553 |
| Walking | Constant_outer Nagoya | 6.059 | 5.519 |
| | Constant_same zonal_inner Nagoya | 6.143 | 3.439 |
| | Constant_same zonal_outer Nagoya | 4.781 | 2.273 |
| | Travel time(min) | -1.870 | |
| | Number of samples | 4,978 | |
| | Log likelihood at zero | -7,973.3 | |
| | Log likelihood at convergence | -4,306.4 | |
| | Adjusted McFadden's Rho-squared | 0.456 | |

*1: These parameter are set beforehand

*2: Representative station is 1 if the station of access side is express stop station, otherwise is 0

*3: Average parking charge (monthly/20days) in destination is calculated from the PT survey data

** All estimated values are different from 0 with 5% statistical significant level

**Table 2.** Total number of class in multi-class combined equilibrium model

| | 1 | 2 | 3 | 4 | 5 | 6 | 7 | 8 | 9 | 10 | 11 |
|---|---|---|---|---|---|---|---|---|---|---|---|
| Job | Worker | | | | | | | | | | Student |
| Gender | Man | | | | | Woman | | | | | - |
| License | O | | | x | | O | | | x | | - |
| Owner | O | | x | O | x | O | | x | O | x | - |
| Type | EV | Gasoline | - | Gasoline | - | EV | Gasoline | - | Gasoline | - | - |

From the estimation results of parameters, we have to divide travelers into 9 classes; workers (sex and with/without driver's license and own car) and students. In addition, we assume an EV owner is a worker and has also driver's license, therefore the total number of class is 11 (see Table.2). If a traveler drives an EV, the travel cost would be reduced substantially because the price of electricity gets much cheaper than that of gasoline. Each travel cost is the product of the OD distance and the basic unit, which is set as EV is 2.0 JPY/km and a general gasoline car is 15.0 JPY/km according to the statistics data concerning the efficiency of fuel consumption [12], thus EV owners might be induced. On the other hand, the other characteristics of EV such as a noise-free vehicle or a restriction of cruising range cannot be clearly considered in this study.

## 3    Impact of Penetration Level of EV to Urban Traffic and Environmental Improvement

### 3.1    Model Validation

The model set up with the parameters estimated in the previous section was applied to the Nagoya Metropolitan Area (about 40 km sphere around Nagoya City). The road network consists of 22,466 links and 7,606 nodes. We use a BPR type link performance function with parameters recently estimated in Japan [13].OD trips in this study consist of the commuting traffic in each class estimated in previous study [14] and the freight car traffic extracted from the census data conducted in 1999.

The total numbers of OD trips for commuting to work or school are 5.99 million and the share of car is 52 % as shown in Fig. 2. Furthermore, with a correlation coefficient of 0.66 and a regression coefficient of 1.14, the reproducibility of the car link flow is relatively good.

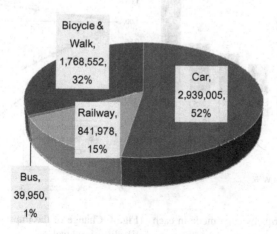

**Fig. 2.** Modal split of the commuting traffic

## 3.2    Impact of EVs to Urban Traffic and Environmental Improvement

In order to assess the impact of the EV spread, the change of mode share and CO2 emissions are calculated in the cases the diffusion rate increase from 5 to 50%. From the change of trips of each mode in Fig.3, it is shown that the car usage increases in response to the penetration level of EV because the fuel cost of EV decreases greatly than that of general gasoline car. On the other hand, the degree of car increasing is very small, and the mode share in each penetration rate does not change so much. In the case of the EV diffusion rate is 10 %, the share of car rises only 0.3 points (i.e. 52.6% → 52.9%) although the shift from railway to EV increases about 20,000 trips.

Fig.4 depicts the change of the vehicle-kilometers, the total travel time, CO2 and NOx emissions as the impact indexes to urban traffic and enviromental inprovement. Here EVs are assumed to emit no pollutants while running, but in this study CO2 emissions in charging the battery of EV add as the extra electrical power generation. CO2 and NOx emissions of EV and the gasoline car are calculated respectively by traffic volume and the basic unit as shown in Table.3.

From Fig.4, the vehicle-kilometers traveled and the total travel time (vehicle-hours traveled) increase in response to the penetration level of EV as the results of reduction of EV's travel cost. As CO2 and NOx emissions are decreased owing to the EV spread, the promotion of EVs can confirm the contribution to the environmental improvement. For example CO2 emissions decrease by 4% in the case the penetration rate of EVs is 10%. In addition, it is desirable to introduce several TDM (transportation and travel demand management) policies including of road pricing aiming at a decrease of car traffic.

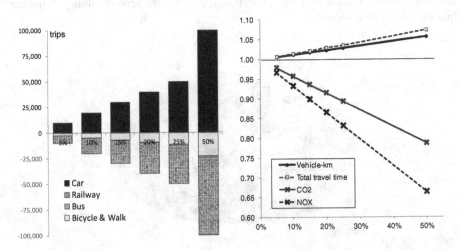

**Fig. 3.** Change of trips by each mode in each EV diffusion level

**Fig. 4.** Change of the impact indexes in each EV diffusion level

**Table 3.** Basic unit of environmental emissions [15] [16] [17]

| | | EV | Gasoline car |
|---|---|---|---|
| $CO_2$ [g/km] | in running | — | $1353.01 \times 1/(spd) -2.7243 \times (spd) +0.02264 \times (spd)^2 +183.809$ |
| | in charging | 51.5 | — |
| NOx [g/km] | in running | — | $-0.902 \times 1/(spd) -5.78 \times 10^{-3} \times (spd) +4.39 \times 10^{-5} \times (spd)^2 +0.261$ |

*spd: average speed in each road link [km/h]

# 4 Evaluation of EV Lanes and EV/Toll Lanes

## 4.1 Set of EV Lanes in the Nagoya Metropolitan Area

The special lanes for EVs would provide the benefit of a reduction of travel time. In this study, in order to compare the effects of EV lanes, three network patterns that are 1) Loop type, 2) Radial type and 3) Integrated type are introduced for the commuting traffics in the Nagoya metropolitan area. The number of lanes in the special network is one, and the road conditions (the regulatory speed etc.) are the same as the competing link. The vehicle which can run in these special lanes is only EV, and interrelated influence with the bus does not consider even if it is a bus route.

< Loop type >          < Radial type >

< Integrated type >

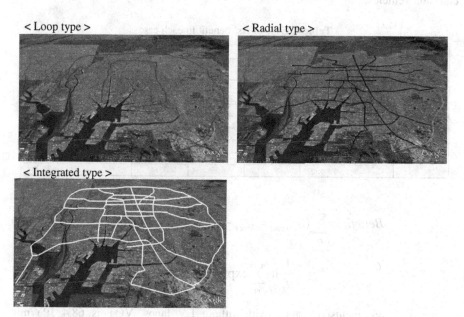

**Fig. 5.** Special lanes for EVs in Nagoya City

## 4.2    Evaluation of EV Lanes

With the introduction of EV lanes in the case EV's diffusion rate is 10%, there is no significant change in modal split and CO2 emissions in all type (Loop, Radial and Integrated). In the case of Integrated type the vehicle-kilometers and the total travel time decreased by 2 % and 4 % respectively compared to the situation in Nagoya city that the penetration rate of EVs is 10 %. Because the travel time for non-EV drivers increases due to capacity decline in road network by introduction of EV lanes, some of them switch to railway (The number of car users decreases by about 10,000 trips in the Integrated type). As a result CO2 emissions in Nagoya city decrease by 3 %.

Table 4 shows EV usage and the EV owners' benefit in each case. Although the utilization ratio of EV is about 71% in all cases, there is slightly difference by the shape of EV lanes. Now, the motive to own EV is assumed to be calculated by the difference value of the EV owner and non-owner of the inclusive value (logsum term) in a nested logit model as shown in formula (3). This is the utility including a decrease of the travel time and costs converted into a money term by the value of time. The EV owners' benefit raises by the introduction of EV lanes, especially the incentive in the case of Integrated type is 473.8 JPY/owner, and 38.4 JPY/owner is higher than before introduction of EV lanes. The annual incentive in this type would be 118,000 JPY/owner (473.8 × 250 days), thus the EV lanes' effects cannot be disregarded although that is smaller than the subsidy or the tax reduction for the low-emission vehicles.

**Table 4.** EV owners' benefit in each case

| | | | EV diffusion rate : 10% | | | |
|---|---|---|---|---|---|---|
| | | Without | Loop (a) | Radial (b) | Integrate (a)+(b) | EV/Toll [200 JPY] |
| EV Usage | EV Owners (person) | 382,435 | 382,435 | 382,435 | 382,435 | 382,435 |
| | EV Users (person) | 269,742 | 270,209 | 271,610 | 272,044 | 270,491 |
| | ratio of utilization | 70.5% | 70.7% | 71.0% | 71.1% | 70.7% |
| EV owners' benefit | Total (Mil. JPY) | 166.5 | 171.1 | 176.5 | 181.2 | 171.4 |
| | pre Owner (JPY) | 435.4 | 447.4 | 461.6 | 473.8 | 448.1 |
| | Effect (-Without) | | 12.0 | 26.2 | 38.4 | 12.7 |
| | per User (JPY) | 617.3 | 633.2 | 649.9 | 666.1 | 633.6 |
| | Effect (-Without) | | 15.9 | 32.6 | 48.8 | 16.3 |

$$Benefit = \sum_{rs} (S^{i,rs}_{without\ EV\ lanes} - S^{i,rs}_{with\ EV\ lanes}) \cdot q^{i,rs}_{EV} \cdot VOT \qquad (3a)$$

$$S^{i,rs} = -\frac{1}{\theta^i_2} \ln \sum_m \exp[-\theta^i_2(V^{i,rs}_m + S^{i,rs}_m)] \qquad (3b)$$

where $S^{i,rs}$ are inclusive values with/without EV lanes, VOT is 68.4 JPY/min calculated in 2.3.

## 4.3    Evaluation of EV/Toll Lanes

The introduction of EV lanes provides an environmental improvement effects in Nagoya city, and also creates an enough incentive effects. However, it would be an inefficient policy because EV owners are not the majority in the metropolitan and the mostly of travelers cannot use the special lanes. Fig. 6 shows the speed fall from the regulatory speed on each link of EV lanes in the case of Integrated type. From this figure we can confirm the congestion level is greatly different in the link of EV lanes, because the speed-fall in the case of special lanes introduced is about 5.0 km/h, in contrast in the base case is about 15.0 km/h.

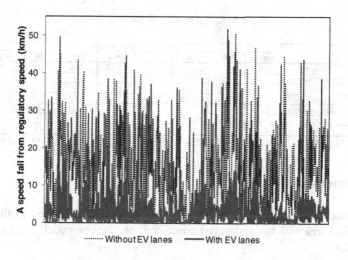

**Fig. 6.** Speed fall on each link of EV lanes

In this study, we propose the EV/Toll lanes in which the EV lanes are opened up to all drivers as the effective use of the road network. However, so as not to cancel out the both effects of environmental improvement and incentives to own an EV, the toll to use the EV lanes is imposed on non-EV drivers. This complies with the policy of HOT lanes proposed as utilization of HOV lanes.

In order to decide a suitable toll level for EV/Toll lanes, we compare the social surplus. The toll sets gradually 8 patterns (i.e. 50, 100, 150, 200, 250, 300, 400 and 500 JPY/enter). Moreover, the object network is the Integrated EV lanes and the diffusion rate of EVs is 10%. Table 5 shows the social surplus in each toll level, which consists of the user benefit, the revenue and $CO_2$ emissions. In the case of the pure EV lanes, EV owners enjoy the benefits of the reductions in travel time and travel cost, but EV non-owners and truck lose their benefits. As a result, social surplus goes negative, and the EV lanes would be judged as inefficient policy. In the EV/Toll lanes, the benefit of EV non-owner remains minus but it is improved well due to the effects of travel time reduction more than paying toll. In addition the benefit of EV owners is a plus, and revenue increase, then the social surplus turns positive. Judging from a viewpoint of the maximization of the social surplus, the toll level of the EV/Toll lane is 200 JPY per enter in this study, and the revenue of charge is 44 million JPY. This revenue could be redistributed to the maintenance of the special lanes, and transport policies for the low-carbon society such as a purchase supports of the low-emission vehicles, an improvement of quick recharge stations for  or a discount of the railway fare.

Here, the effect of incentive creation for the EV owner is confirmed in Table 4. The incentive in the EV/Toll lanes with 200 JPY/enter is 448.1 JPY/owner, and 12.7 JPY/owner is higher than before introduction of EV lanes. Furthermore, $CO_2$ and NOx emissions in Nagoya city decrease by 3 % and 4 % respectively.

**Table 5.** Social surplus in EV/Toll lanes

Unit : Mil.JPY/Peak hours in Morning

| | | Toll level [JPY/enter] | | | | | | | | |
|---|---|---|---|---|---|---|---|---|---|---|
| | | Nothing | 50 | 100 | 150 | 200 | 250 | 300 | 400 | 500 |
| User Benefit | EV Owner | 12.07 | 0.69 | 1.88 | 3.10 | 3.93 | 4.65 | 5.35 | 6.59 | 7.78 |
| | EV non-Owner | -42.41 | -11.03 | -13.83 | -14.34 | -15.94 | -18.43 | -21.43 | -27.18 | -31.25 |
| | Truck | -9.86 | -2.58 | -3.68 | -4.56 | -5.41 | -6.16 | -6.98 | -8.35 | -9.46 |
| Revenue | Fare (mass transit) | 3.45 | 0.98 | 1.16 | 1.27 | 1.47 | 1.67 | 1.88 | 2.27 | 2.56 |
| | Toll (Expressway) | 5.90 | -0.81 | -1.49 | -2.67 | -1.80 | -0.93 | -0.43 | -0.15 | 0.89 |
| | Charge | 0.00 | 23.42 | 34.10 | 41.47 | 43.75 | 45.06 | 45.26 | 42.48 | 37.50 |
| Emission | CO2 | -0.01 | 0.06 | 0.07 | 0.05 | 0.06 | 0.05 | 0.04 | 0.04 | 0.03 |
| Social Surplus | | -30.87 | 10.72 | 18.22 | 24.32 | 26.05 | 25.91 | 23.70 | 15.69 | 8.04 |

# 5     Conclusion

We evaluate the effects of EV lanes and EV/Toll lanes introduced in the Nagoya metropolitan area with the multi-class combined equilibrium model. The key findings are as follows:

(1)    The impacts of EVs to an environmental improvement are quantitatively shown. From the evaluation results of the EV lanes, there is no significant change in the metropolitan area, but in Nagoya city, the vehicle-kilometers traveled and the total travel time decreased by 2 % and 4 % respectively, and $CO_2$ emissions decrease by 3 %.

(2)    The incentive to own an EV is 473.8 JPY/owner and 38.4 JPY/owner is higher than before introduction of EV lanes (integrated type). However the social surplus is minus.

(3)    The social surplus in the EV/Toll lanes is greatly improved by charging 200 JPY per enter on a general gasoline car. And $CO_2$ emissions decreases by 4%.

(4)    It is expected that the EV spread advances more by redistributing the revenue of the EV/Toll lanes to a new purchase subsidy or the quick recharge stations, etc.

**Acknowledgments.** This research was supported by the Environment Research and Technology Development Fund (E-1003) of the Ministry of the Environment, Japan and the Funding Program for Next Generation World-Leading Researchers (NEXT Program) of Cabinet office.

# References

1. Green, R.C., Wang, L., Alam, M.: The impact of plug-in hybrid electric vehicles on distribution networks: A review and outlook. Renewable and Sustainable Energy Reviews 15, 544–553 (2011)
2. Nesanani, K.S., Chu, L., Recker, W.: Policy Implications of Incorporating Hybrid Vehicles into High-Occupancy Vehicle Lanes. Journal of Transportation Systems Engineering and Information Technology 10, 30–41 (2010)
3. Yang, H., Huang, H.-J.: Carpooling and congestion pricing in a multilane highway with high-occupancy vehicle lanes. Transportation Research Part A 33, 139–155 (1999)
4. Konishi, H., Mun, S.: Carpooling and Congestion Pricing: HOV and HOT Lanes. Regional Science and Urban Economics 40, 173–186 (2010)
5. Kwon, J., Varaiya, P.: Effectiveness of California's High Occupancy Vehicle (HOV) system. Transportation Research Part C 16, 98–115 (2008)
6. Ecola, L., Light, T.: Making Congestion Pricing Equitable. Transportation Research Record 2187, 53–59 (2011)
7. Ben-Akiva, M., Lerman, S.R.: Discrete Choice Analysis: Theory and Application to Travel Demand. The MIT Press (1985)
8. Fisk, C.: Some developments in equilibrium traffic assignment. Transportation Research Part B 14, 243–255 (1980)
9. Boyce, D., Bar-Gera, H.: Multiclass Combined Models for Urban Travel Forecasting. Networks and Spatial Economics 4, 115–124 (2004)
10. Akamatsu, T.: Decomposition of Path Choice Entropy in General Transport Networks. Transportation Science 31, 349–362 (1997)
11. Miwa, T., Sakai, T., Morikawa, T.: Route Identification and Travel Time Prediction Using Probe-Car Data. International Journal of ITS Research 2, 21–28 (2004)
12. Next Generation Vehicle Promotion Center, http://www.cev-pc.or.jp/index.html
13. Yoshida, Y., Ishiya, M., Harata, N.: Estimation of the Link Cost Function by Using the Yearly Traffic Observation. Traffic Engineering 40, 80–89 (2005) (in Japanese)
14. Kanamori, R.: Estimation of Residence-Workplace Population Distribution by Individual Attributes Under Relaxation of One-side's Population Constraints. In: Proceedings of Infrastructure Planning, vol. 42 CD-ROM (2010) (in Japanese)
15. Oshiro, N., Oneyama, H., Yamada, T., Ohnishi, H.: Emission Factors of Vehicles for Air Pollution Prediction near Highways. Civil Engineering Journal 42, 60–63 (2000) (in Japanese)
16. Oshiro, N., Mathusita, M., Namikawa, Y., Ohnishi, H.: Fuel Consumption and Emission Factors of Carbon Dioxide for Motor Vehicle. Civil Engineering Journal 43, 50–55 (2001) (in Japanese)
17. Federation of Electric Power Companies, http://www.fepc.or.jp/index.html

# Simulation of Coordinated Anticipatory Vehicle Routing Strategies on MATSim⋆

Enrique de la Hoz, Ivan Marsa-Maestre, and Miguel A. Lopez-Carmona

Computer Engineering Department, Universidad de Alcala
Escuela Politecnica, 28871, Alcala de Henares (Madrid), Spain
{enrique.delahoz,ivan.marsa,miguelangel.lopez,pablo.perez}@uah.es

**Abstract.** During the last years, a great variety of simulation tools have been developed to analyze transportation scenarios. In spite of this effort, there are no vehicle traffic simulator that integrate in a realistic way communication techniques in these scenarios. Moreover, on-the-fly re-routing during the simulation is usually not supported. In this work we present an extension to the multiagent simulator MATSim that enables both features and makes it possible to simulate coordinated anticipatory vehicle routing strategies. Finally, some basic replanning strategies, which make use of this capabilities, are simulated and some preliminary results are shown.

## 1 Introduction

Throughout all modern industrialized economies we can see evidence of the importance of road transportation. As the number of vehicles to be accommodated increases and the scope to build new and bigger motorways decreases, we witness a climb in traffic congestion despite current efforts to free the flow of traffic. It is estimated that traffic congestion costs about 1% of European Union Gross Domestic Product [1] . Average mobility per person in the EU, measured in passenger-kilometre per inhabitant, increased by 7% between 2000 and 2008, mainly through higher motorisation levels as well as more high-speed rail and air travel. New vehicles have become more fuel efficient and hence emit less $CO_2$ per km than earlier models did in the past, but these gains have been eaten up by rising vehicle numbers, increasing traffic volumes, and in many cases better performance in terms of speed, safety and comfort. All this figures clearly show not only how traffic is already a very serious problem but also that is growing so it becomes unavoidable trying to find new solutions to address this situation in nowadays societies taking into account, also, the growing concerns about sustainability and emission reductions in both modern and developing countries.

Collecting and delivering real-time information to urban traffic control centers can help infrastructure operators manage traffic more efficiently, potentially reducing standstill traffic and congestion by up to 40% with equivalent

⋆ This work has been supported by the Spanish Ministry of Education and Science grant TIN2008-06739-C04-04.

S. Cranefield and I. Song (Eds.): PRIMA 2011 Workshops, LNAI 7580, pp. 90–108, 2012.
© Springer-Verlag Berlin Heidelberg 2012

energy savings [15]. Next generation Intelligent Transportation Systems (ITS) attempt to integrate information and communications technologies with the existing transportation infrastructure and vehicles in order to reduce traffic congestion, improve safety, reduce vehicle wear, etc [6]. ITSs such as traffic network management systems take data from sensors which are constantly observing road network conditions and then use this information to decide on the best action to take (e.g. change traffic light signal) in order to optimize the flow of traffic, thus increasing efficiency in road management and reducing traffic congestion. It is recognised that the future of ICT applications in transport for safety and efficiency lay in cooperative systems, based on vehicle-to-vehicle and vehicle-to-infrastructure communications, rather than in autonomous systems

One of the most important example of ITS are navigation systems. Aside from basic navigation systems, which use static maps for the fastest path routing, more advanced devices exploit broadcast traffic information. Following this kind of approaches, navigation systems are able to reroute according to real-time traffic conditions. For example, an accident that causes a traffic jam on the route of a vehicle can trigger the vehicle to reroute an bypass the traffic jam. These mechanisms allow a substantial performance gain when compared with static routing.

One disadvantage of the state-of-the-art approaches is that they allow us to react upon traffic jams after they have occurred and, hence, already propagate delays in a typically substantial part of the traffic network. Anticipatory vehicle routing aims at encompassing this approach by using forecast of traffic density. Forecast information can either be extracted from historical data or directly rely on the individual planned routes of the vehicles. Another disadvantage of current approaches is that only the maximisation of individual utility is considered, with no particular allowance made for holistic social utility. Currently, car navigation systems encourages users to take the shortest route derived from traffic information known, monitored through vehicle information and communication systems. When you see and individual not paying attention to social utility, most of the car agents adopt the same traffic information. This inevitably causes heavy congestion. Coordinated anticipatory vehicle routing deals with this issue by taking into account when suggesting potential routes information from as many vehicles as possible trying to find a compromise between individual goals and social utility.

A key element to this development process is simulation of vehicular networks. Traffic simulation is necessary because this kind of application domain is inherently complex, usually formed of diverse entities (vehicles, traffic controllers, pedestrians, etc.) that present different interactions reflecting social behaviours (e.g. competition, collaboration) and thus mathematical analyses are complex and deal with traffic as a whole, using flow equations to describe vehicles and pedestrian movements. Moreover, simulation can provide comparison studies between new infrastructures or controls without interfering in the real system or spending resources.

Transportation and traffic science classifies traffic models into Macroscopic and Microscopic models, according to the granularity with which traffic flows are examined. Accordingly, simulation methodologies fall into two main categories; macro simulation and micro simulation. In macro simulations, the subjects are modeled from the macroscopic viewpoint and expressed using governing equations. While the macro simulation methodology is suitable for the analysis of physical phenomena because its foreseeable and uniform mechanisms, it is not suitable to replicate the social phenomena that emerge from human-human interactions due to the imprecise nature of human decision-making mechanisms. For the latter, micro simulations are to be preferred. Micro simulations allow each entity to be distinctly represented so we can replicate societies consisting of humans in a natural way.

Multiagent-based simulation is a version of micro-simulation. Multiagent-based simulation yields multiagent societies that well reproduce human societies, and so are seen as an excellent tool for analyzing the real world. In a multiagent-based simulation, crowd behaviour can emerge though interactions among agents while each agent can be impacted by the emerging behaviour.

One prominent example of a multiagent-based simulator is the MATSim simulator. In this paper we propose an extension for the MATSim simulator to enable the simulation of coordinated anticipatory vehicle routing (CAVR) algorithms. To illustrate these capabilities, some basic replanning strategies for anticipatory and coordinated anticipatory vehicle routing are shown.

The rest of the paper is organized as follows. Section 3 presents MATSim and the within day functionality. Section 4 focuses on the modifications introduced in the simulator. Section 5 presents a basic anticipatory vehicle routing strategy that employs some of the features added to the simulator. Section 6 is devoted to simulation of the strategy and analysis of the results obtained. Section 1 shows a proposal for Coordinated Anticipatory Vehicle Routing and presents some results of its simulation taking advantage of the capabilities added to MATSim. Finally, section 8 summarizes our conclusions and proposes some lines of future work.

## 2    Simulation of Coordinated Anticipatory Routing Strategies

The U.S. National Intelligent Transportation Systems (ITS)[1] outlines an evolution in route guidance architectures. The first step of this evolution is an autonomous architecture in which all vehicles make isolated decisions based on static link data. This autonomous architecture is followed by a decentralized architecture in which real-time information is broadcast to vehicles, allowing them to adjust their routing to current traffic densities. The third and final step would be a centralized architecture in which vehicles send routing requests to an Independent Service Provider (ISP). This ISP will then provide the vehicle with an individualized route, taking into account all other issued routes to predict future traffic states. Such a centralized architecture is expected to solve the

---

[1] http://www.iteris.com/itsarch/

problems predicted in [25]. In [25], the authors argue that providing information to vehicles can lead to instability and inefficient decision making as all vehicles take part in a minority game. The need for this last evolution, i.e., the transition from a decentralized to centralized architecture, can be avoided by providing the vehicles with predictive, instead of real-time, information, according to [27].

The physical process brought about by a particular situation where agents, sharing the same information, are urged to compete for a limited resource (traffic capacity, service capacity, etc) is called the common resource distribution problem, of which known derivations are the Minority Game or El farol bar Problem [21] . The most important key for solving this kind of problem is knowing how to maintain the probabilistic deviation of an agents' action. In [21], for example, authors propose an advanced strategic form of shortest time routing where only partial information is shared among the agents.

There is already an extensive body of work that involves the term CVR. [8] and [27] propose CVR based on delegate multiagent systems and biologically inspired algorithms. The cooperative car navigation system proposed in [28] is based on route information sharing. Here, each vehicle transmits route information to a route information server, which estimates future traffic congestion and feeds this estimate back to each vehicle. However, the minority game problem is not considered here, and each vehicle reroute individually.

Propagation of information through traffic networks using biologically inspired mechanisms such as pheromones or swarms have extensively been studied by [3] and by [22]. Propagation of information using swarm intelligence as in [8] resembles Reservation-Based Mechanisms [10,24].

From the perspective of control theory, controlling a large-scale system such as an urban road traffic system is not a trivial task due to its unpredictability and uncertainty [23]. The optimal control of flows in any traffic network, including road traffic networks, is a well known non-deterministic polynomial-time (NP)-hard problem. Traditional control techniques usually consist of an off-line search for the best control strategy for typical situations that traffic planners faced in the past. Unfortunately, fluctuations in dynamic systems are usually huge, and therefore, the resulting control strategy is optimized for a situation that is true on average but than never occurs at any single instant. To tackle this problem, a computationally viable option is an online and distributed control strategy.

In recent years, there has been increasing interest in applying agent-based techniques for traffic control, whose appeal stems from their composite nature, flexibility, and scalability. In [17], a self-organizing approach is presented, which leads to emergent coordination patterns and achieves an efficient decentralized control. Other approaches focus on the behavioural modeling of drivers [2,20]. Congestion charges are another mechanism to influence the driver behaviour, which are aimed at penalizing drivers for the externalities that they cause to other drivers (congestion) and to the environment (pollution). In [13], authors propose the optimal coordination of variable speed limits and ramp metering in a freeway network, where the objective of the control is to minimize the total time that the vehicles spend in the network. In [11], a control system for traffic signals is proposed which is based on vehicle route sharing. The shared information is used for calculating the expected traffic congestion as in [28]).

Simulations with multiagent systems (MASs) based approaches and biologically inspired algorithms using forecast data, even when gathered in a decentralized manner, helps drivers reach their destination up to 35% faster, compared with drivers who use no data or real-time data made available by Traffic Message Channel (TMC) services. The forecast data not only allow drivers to avoid existing congestion but prevents them from forming congestion as well. However, providing efficient and stable routes to vehicles is challenging, even with forecast data, as these techniques are applied to larger traffic scenarios that involve more dynamics. Further experimentation with learning algorithms could improve the quality of predictive information. Computational market approaches usually exhibit the previously mentioned problems as well: infrastructures to provide such services are not considered in the proposals, these systems are hard to understand, and because of that, it is not clear the acceptability of such systems by the users. Regarding model predictive control approaches their main limitations are in their scalability, and in the formulation and application of traffic models that more accurately represent traffic flow. We believe that the behavioural, social holistic utility, communication technologies and simplicity should be considered in a more coordinated way in order to build appealing advanced routing applications. Anyway, we should think about why these approaches are still not in our roads. Besides, no existing vehicle traffic simulation platform can provide the power and sophistication needed for the simulation of CAVR algorithms.

Although a variety of simulation tools has been developed to analyze transportation scenarios at the micro- and macro-scale levels and in the last years, little effort has been devoted to the integration of communication techniques and scenarios in a realistic transportation simulation environment [19]. On-the-fly rerouting during the simulation has hardly been a topic for research. According to [5], there are two main reasons. First, there is a correspondence between routes and strategies that an agent may choose (game theoretic analysis). As long as they cannot create a new strategy on the fly, they cannot modify the set of known routes as a result of a new strategy being learned. Second, different states of the traffic simulation problem are managed by different tools: travel demand generation, route choice and driving simulation are usually modeled as steps that are under the control of different software packages. As a matter of a fact, existing simulators do not support the dynamic modification of the vehicles route [5] or do it in a very limited way when some integration with network simulators (Omnet++, ns-2) is provided as in [26][12].

When it comes to traffic simulators, with no network simulator integration, none of the existing traffic simulators complies with the requirements imposed by these scenarios [19]. Nevertheless, MATSim[2] (Multi-Agent Transport Simulation) has some basic functionalities, namely *within-day replanning* modules [9][14] developed by C. Dobler[3]. Within day replanning module in MATSim

---

[2] http://www.matsim.org
[3] http://www.matsim.org/node/587

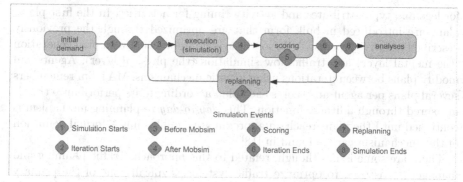

**Fig. 1.** Simulation process of MATSim

extends MATSim to allow to incorporate modifications to the planned routes of the vehicles during the simulation. However, there exists neither support for agent communication nor any aid to group formation or agent filtering. Given that these features are a requirement when agent coordination or cooperation are to be simulated, we decided to implement them as a contribution to the existing MATSim core.

## 3 MATSim

MATSim (Multi-Agent Transport Simulation) is a framework for iterative, agent-based microsimulations of transport systems that is currently developed by teams at ETH Zurich and TU Berlin. It consists of several modules that can be used independently or as part of the framework.[4] provides a detailed description of the framework. Because of its agent-based approach, each person in the system is modeled as an individual agent in the simulated scenario. Each of these agents has personalized parameters such as age, sex, available transport modes and scheduled activities per day. Due to the modular structure of the simulation framework, the agent's parameters can be easily extended with new parameters, for example for the routing strategy that should be used or the areas of the road network that the agent knows.

MATSim tries to optimize travel demand to meet the challenges of simulating large scenarios. The demand optimization, which is shown in Fig.1, is an evolutionary process. The optimized demand can only be analyzed after many iterations of the loop (execution, scoring and replanning) shown in Fig. 1. The traffic simulation (execution) generates events for each action in the simulation (e.g. link enter) that are then processed as part of the simulation process.

One of the key aspects of MATSim is demand modeling. In MATSim, every agent has its own *plan*, which contains both the intended schedule for the agent (*activities*) and the travel *legs* connecting the activities. Both legs and activities may hold several attributes, describing the travel from one activity to another such as departure time, expected arrival time, route and transportation mode for legs and type attributes and activity timing for activities. In the first place, plans are introduced in bulk form that are optimized through the previously described iterative process. To do so, the system iterates between plan generation (the mental layer) and traffic flow simulation (the physical layer). Agents can modify plans between iterations using genetic mechanisms. MATSim remembers several plans per agent and scores each plan according to its performance that is measured through a fitness function. This *day-to-day* re-planning mechanism is continued until the plans reach an approximate equilibrium. A formal definition of this mechanism can be found in [18].

There are some issues though, related to this approach. Traffic planning and management is used to optimize traffic systems. Typically one of the primary tasks of planning activities is to design, adapt or manage traffic systems in a way that in common situations their load remains below a justifiable level. Simulating such a scenario can be achieved using an iterative approach. As long as only typical, repetitive situations are modeled, iterative can produce meaningful. The adaptable parameters of the scenario, for example the plans of the agents, are optimized until the simulation model reaches an equilibrium. The approach can be validated with interviews to individuals. If they typically got stuck in a traffic jam on a certain link every morning, they will probably avoid being there in the future.

On the other hand a scenario may also contain incidents that occur by chance, which increases the complexity of the needed model significantly. If this is the case, an iterative approach could be seen as inappropriate. This can be illustrated with a simple example. In an iterative approach, if a road gets blocked suddenly because of, for instance, an accident, in the first iteration the agents, which do not know about the accident yet, may choose routes that contain the road affected by the accident. Thus, those agents will get stuck. For the next iteration, agents will take this information into account and will replan its routes accordingly so they will probably choose another route. As iterations go by, more agents will avoid blocked road so it could be the case that in the end nobody will travel over that road after it got blocked, and thus the traffic jam that every agent is trying to avoid simply will not exist.

When we are to simulate this kind of scenarios, we should take into consideration that there are a whole group of events that cannot be foreseen. Although some kind of proactive behaviour can be assumed for agents, they cannot predict accurately every possible situation, even if the incident is predictable, up to some extent (e.g., accidents tend to happen in some troubled links). Agents may have some partial knowledge but they cannot know it as accurate as they do after several iterations of the simulation. Thus, to provide more accurate results for scenarios with this kind of constraints, it seems wiser not to use an iterative approach but an approach able to react to incidents once they have occurred. To do so, we should be able to create agent's routes on the fly while they are travelling. This approach is called *within day replanning* to make explicit the differences with the usual day-to-day replanning approach.

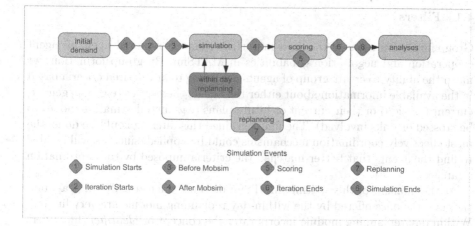

**Fig. 2.** Within Day Replanning in MATSim

Within day replanning has been pointed as useful in urban scenarios such as taxi distribution [7] and park search and also in large scale events like accidents, disasters and evacuations [16]. Although when using within day replanning it is possible to introduce en-route modifications in the agent's plan, the existing implementation does not allow to exchange any information among agents or with the infrastructure to take into account additional information, more than the one an agent is able to retrieve, to compute those modifications to the pre-existing plan. Moreover, there is no mechanism to allow agents to communicate with each other. Without this, neither route coordination mechanism nor route suggestions can be studied.

The required modifications can be grouped as follows:

- *Message passing capabilities*: allowing agents to generate messages containing any kind of information and address them to either individual agents or groups.
- *Filtering capabilities*: one of the key aspects of any coordination strategy is the formation of groups. Filtering capabilities should permit a straight and easy formation of groups according to any desired criteria.
- *Modelling network state*: although MATSim core contains information about the state of the network, there was not an easy way to provide agents with this information. This is definitely a requirement given that agents need to know in advance about the state of the links in order to make smart re-route decisions. Partial or total knowledge should be modeled.

## 4  Extending MATSim

One of the contribution of this paper is to provide MATSim with the necessary capabilities so that dynamic en-route plan modifications can be simulated. In this section we describe the main modifications that have been introduced in the simulator.

## 4.1  Filters

Group formation is one of the most important elements required to enable agent cooperation and negotiation capabilities in MATSim. By group formation, we mean the ability to create group of agents according to any desired criteria based in the available information about either the agents themselves (e.g, age, gender, current position) or their current or future plans (e.g. final destination, nodes to be crossed or links involved). The finest-grained this filtering could be done, the most effectively coordination mechanisms could be applied, since we will be able to find the agents that better matched the criteria imposed by the coordination strategies.

At the moment of this writing, MATSim does not offer any filtering capabilities, and the ones offered by the within-day replanning module are very limited. Within day replanning module incorporates the concept of *identifier*. Identifiers are classes used to filter a set of agents that matches some constraint defined by the programmer to enforce replanning of their current routes. In within day replanning only the agents that satisfy some criteria get their plan rescheduled.

Although this could seem quite similar to the goal exposed in the first paragraph, there are important differences being the most important of them what the agents are filtered for. Identifiers allow the selection of a subset of agents solely for replanning purposes. However, we envision a more flexible scenario where group formation is not only tied to the exact replanning instant but to all the required process that drives the agent to it: communication, exchange of proposals and decision making.

With these goals in mind, we propose the introduction of a generic filtering mechanism in MATSim. This filtering mechanisms allows the programmer to create sets of agents according to any constraint. The filtering mechanism relies on a static class, `Filters`, which has as attributes a list containing all the network agents and a `NetSim` object to access network information. Building upon these, any filtering mechanisms can be built in the form of a member function that in its simplest form would be the `all()` method where no filtering is performed.

Of special interest for route replanning is the formation of groups based on the agent's route information. We can think of a scenario where a link is experimenting a growing congestion. A smart algorithm would try to prevent the appearance of more severe problems by routing temporarily the agents that would be to transverse that link or a set of them. The right decision would not be to re-route every agent that had that link in its route plan but a subset of them. For instance, to avoid a faster growing of congestion, the agents that are to enter that link and also would be some of the agents that are more than one link away could be enforced to re-route. The decisions of which agents to re-route may be made according to an inverse proportionality law and the behavioural model of each agent.

To implement this strategy, we could form at least two groups, one with the agents that are about to enter the link, and another with the agents that should cross the link after two or more steps. While the first one, where every agent gets replanned, would be equivalent if identifiers would be used, the second one, where only a subset of them will be replanned following some kind of agreement among them, shows the need for the mechanism we are proposing.

To fulfil this need, a mechanism to perform agent filtering based on the presence of a node, link in agent's plan or any fixed-length portion of it has been implemented.

## 4.2    Network Status

Although MATSim itself provides a representation of the information of every link in the network through `NetSim` objects, we have decided to implement a new interface to access that information to ease down both access and the inherent network complexity. Using this newly introduced code, agents can easily access network information in a straightforward and simple manner. Current implementation of MATSim tries to isolate agents from direct access to this information.

For the sake of simplicity, only two classes have been implemented. The first one, `NetLink`, models a single link. Its parameters are updated any time an agent enters or leaves that link. The second one, `NetStat`, models the whole network as a set of nodes connected by links, which are in turn modeled as `NetLink` objects. A `NetStat` object is created, usually from the MATSim `Controller` class, and it is initialized from the system-wide variable `netSim`. After that, every time an agent enters or leaves a link, the `NetStat` object is updated accordingly so that it keeps a coherent representation of the network status.

## 4.3    Agent Communication

A key aspect to enable agent cooperation is the ability of agents to communicate among them. We can think not only about route coordination scenarios but also about accident notification or mere information propagation. The main goal governing this module was to provide a framework where any kind of information of any type, that is, not only primitive data types but complex structures, could be exchanged among agents and between agents and the infrastructure. Our proposal supports both unicast and multicast/broadcast communication. By covering both, any possible inter-agent communication scenario is sufficiently managed.

Messages are modeled as objects of the abstract class `Message`. It would be up to each application to create classes for the messages it requires by means of deriving them from `Message` class. The simplest message that could be exchange would be a message that would contain a simple `String`. This could be used to propagate any kind of information (e.g. an accident warning). The class `StringMessage` implements this. Very similar to the previous one, the class `AgentMessage` contains the identification of an agent and could be used for group registration, for instance.

In order to be able to conduct more complex negotiations, new message types must be introduced to represent route and agent information. The two basic elements of this kind are `PlanMessage` and `PlanElement`, the former representing the full activity plan an agent has, and the latter any element of that plan, e.g. an activity or a leg definition or a mere link. As it will be shown later, this would be necessary for route re-planning. Related to these classes, and of great relevance for route replanning is the `CrowdedLink` message type. This message is generates every time an agent enters a link and finds it with a level of congestion greater than a fixed threshold. It will contain the link of set of links that are affected by the congestion situation and will be used to advertise about this situation to other agents. Finally, a message that contains information about the status of the network links has been created. This message is called `NetStat` and it will be used by agents to exchange information about the perceived status of a link or a set of links. This message could also be generated by the existing infrastructure, road side units (RSU) and could advertise link status to all nearby agents.

The inter-agent communication is handled by a newly created class which is called `MessageHandler`. This class provides the agents with methods for sending and receiving messages of any of the previously enumerated types. Also, with the functionality of filters, it manages the group communication features (multicast and broadcast communication).

With our extensions to MATSim regarding filters, network status and agent communication, we can now try to use distributed dynamic en-route replanning strategies to improve vehicle traffic. Some replanning strategies are presented in next sections along with a preliminary study of the effect of such strategies, which is provided in section 6.

## 5  Basic Replanning Strategies

In this section, we propose a basic distributed strategy for route coordination to provide a verification test of the modifications introduced in MATSim. The idea behind this is to show that the described modifications could be used to implement replanning strategies based not only an agent's own information but also in the information received from some group or groups of agents. In spite of the simplicity of the strategy we are about to describe, it shows the key aspects any strategy should consist of, namely a policy for group formation, information sharing and a replanning mechanism.

As we have explained, the strategy we are going to use for this verification purpose is quite simple. Every time and agent enters a link, the congestion state of the link will be checked. If the link congestion is above a fixed threshold, the agent will generate an especially crafted message, `CrowdedLink`, indicating that the link is congested. The agent will send the message to a subset of agents. We will study the results obtained depending on the agents belonging to that group. If the link is not crowded, no message will be generated. After that, a replanning will take place but the replanning will only affect to those agents that have received the previous message. This second filtering does not involve our filtering class but a new identifier class that we have called `MessageCrowdedLinkIdentifier`.

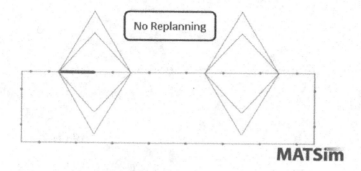

**Fig. 3.** Simple Scenario: no replanning

# 6  Simulation of the Basic Replanning Strategies

This section presents the results of the simulation of the strategy defined in the previous section. Two scenarios have been considered: a simple scenario and a more realistic urban scenario. The simple scenario presents a non-realistic scenario and its presence here is just for the sake of showing the importance of taking into account coordination and cooperation issues when re-routing strategies are to be employed. This is not a individual optimization problem but a more complex global optimization challenge as we will see.

## 6.1  Simple Scenario

As we have explained in the previous paragraph, a simple scenario has been studied to show the importance of coordination. Fig. 3 shows the initial situation when no replanning is performed. The agents are forced to go through the link in the middle when they get to the crossroad and got stuck in that link because is capacity is way smaller than the capacity of the link they were coming from. Given that there seems to be alternate routes that have been almost free of traffic, re-planning could help to avoid congestion.

We conducted an experiment where the replanning strategy described in section 5 is used in combination with the Next Link filter thus congestion will be detected as soon as the link gets crowded and the agents will follow an alternate route. Unfortunately, congestion moves but not disappear because agents will tend to choose the same alternate link and congestion will just move there. Once the alternate link gets crowded itself, the agents will replan again moving to another link that finally will get crowded also. Thus every alternate link will become crowded in a periodic manner. Fig. 4 shows this situation. Some kind of coordination is needed to avoid these undesirable side effects.

Additional replanning strategies were considered by modifying the set of replanning agents (as described in section 5). Thus, the All, Next Link, In Leg and Complete Route 4 (the congested link is four links away from the link the

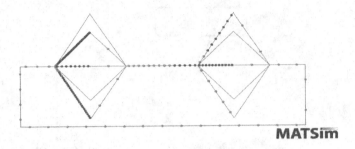

**Fig. 4.** Simple scenario: next link replanning

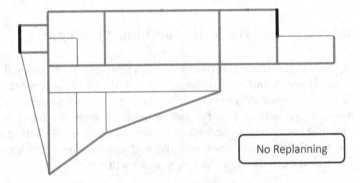

**Fig. 5.** Urban scenario: no replanning

agent is in) strategies were analyzed. The results clearly state that the application of any strategy would offer a great improvement in the average travel time although no strategy is clearly better than the rest because of the simplicity of the network. The complex scenario, which will be analyzed next, will help to shed some light on this.

## 6.2   Urban Scenario

In this case we analyze a more complex scenario that has been specially crafted to recreate a small part of a city. We have considered different kind of roads with different capacity. In Fig. 5, which has been obtained with one of the MATSim's visualizers, the OTFVis tool, it is shown how some vehicles got stuck in some links because of the differences in capacity between adjacent links.

Due to the more complex nature of this network, more alternatives can be taken into account when it comes to replanning. Thus, replanning strategies could contribute more efficiently to congestion reduction. Some experiments have been conducted in this scenario. We have considered the basic replanning strategy applied to different subsets via filters, namely All, Next Link, In Leg,

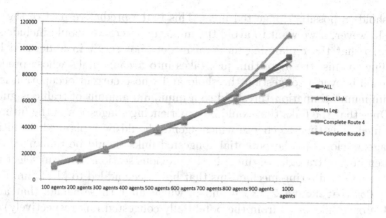

**Fig. 6.** Urban scenario: average travel time

Complete Route 4 and Complete Route 3. Results are shown in Fig. 6. According to the graph, there is a great improvement in average travel time when we introduce some replanning strategy of any kind. Nevertheless, it is only when the number of agents increase when differences among the different mechanisms arise. So we can see how, as expected, the Next Link strategy performs worse than all the other strategies, not only those strategies that try to make replanning decisions with more anticipation as Complete Route 3 or Complete Route 4 but also than All. Also, both strategies perform better than In Leg strategy. Taking re-routing decisions with more anticipation, makes it possible to choose between a wider set of choices for agents redistribution diminishing congestion this way.

# 7 Coordinated Anticipatory Routing Strategies

As we have seen in the previous sections, anticipatory routing seems to offer some improvements as long as we avoid the formation of severe congestion in some links by means of detecting potential problems in some links. Nevertheless, this approach, as it has been pointed earlier, is prone to the minority game resulting on most of the agents avoiding the potential congested link in a way such that in the end not only the link is not congested but it is almost not used.

Coordination strategies have to be taken into account to avoid this problem. Thus, to be able to make efficient re-routing, we should include not only congestion information but also information regarding the routes that agents are about to follow. This way we could predict to some extent the future occupation of the links. We propose the utilization of a centralized approach where agents share their planned routed with a central entity which acts as coordinator. This central entity uses this information to predict the future occupation of the links according to the agents' advertised routes. The algorithm will proceed as follows. First, the coordinator identifies those links such that their potential occupation is over a threshold as possible congested links. This is the predictive part of the algorithm. However, if we want to avoid the minority game, we should include some criteria so that the replanning mechanism does not result in underused links. According to this, the algorithm just takes into account links whose predicted occupation is over a congestion threshold and whose current occupation is also over minimum occupation threshold so a minimum amount of traffic is guaranteed. Once that the links that could be experiencing congestion in the future are determined, it is time to choose which agents should be replanned. Intuitively, those agents closer to the potential congested links should be replanned as we have seen in the strategies outlined in the previous sections. We can select those agents using the filtering mechanisms that have been added to MATSim. Filters such as `CompleteRoute 2, 3, 4` and `5`, which filter those agents that are up to 2, 3, 4 or 5 links away from the potentially congested link respectively) seem quite appropriate for this goal. Again, we will use the `CrowdedLink` message to inform to those agent that they should replan. Those agents who receive that message, will be included in an `identifier`. `Identifiers` are the way to pass group of agents to replan to MATSim replanners.

A realistic simulation of this kind of environments should also include considerations regarding the social adoption of this technologies. On one hand, autonomous driving experiments have shown that drivers are reluctant to accept systems that are able to make up by their own. It is reasonable to believe that autonomous replanning would make drivers feel awkward about what is actually going on behind the scene and not confident about that. To deal with this, a model based on suggestions should be adopted where drivers are presented with some choices showing his potential improvements regarding travel time leaving it to the driver to make the final decision. On the other hand, as with any other technology, it is expected a gradual adoption of this kind of technologies. This way, for a long time there will be vehicles with these technologies sharing the road with others that do not. This has an important impact on the accuracy of the predictions in which our system relies on as long as vehicles without this technology would not be informing about their planned routes. On the contrary, as long as this group will not do any replanning, the minority game problem is somehow alleviated.

We have conducted some preliminary experiments to evaluate the proposed algorithm in a 10 by 10 Manhattan grid scenario. The scenario is shown in Figure 7 We have set a minimum occupation threshold of 20% and a congestion threshold of 60%. The grid has been designed to force the appearance of congestion in the planned route. At the beginning, every agent has been programmed to follow the same route (shortest path) and a number enough of agents has been set up so severe congestion will appear if no replanning is performed. We have conducted experiments under different settings: with no replanning at all( `NoReplanning`), with the basic replanning strategy depicted in section 5 (`Basic`) and with the coordinated anticipatory replanning strategy (`CIwithout6020`).Also, we have evaluated the proposed CAVR strategy under different assumptions about the degree of technology adoption (10% and 30% vehicles not equipped with the technology,

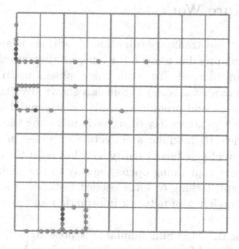

**MATSim**

**Fig. 7.** Manhattan grid scenario

`CIWithoutT10`) and `CIWithoutT30` respectively) and about the probability of acceptance of the suggested routes by the driver (`CIwith6020`, value of probability, 0.5). Results are shown in table 1.

While non-conclusive, some conclusions can be obtained from the results shown in table 1. The proposed strategy leads to an important reduction in travel time both over the basic replanning strategy and no replanning scenarios. This was expected as no coordination was taken into account in the basic replanning strategy and thus being prone to the minority game problem. Also, it should be noted that better results are achieved when not very vehicle follows the suggested routes. This is again related to the minority problem. As long as there are vehicles that should keep on following their pre-planned routes, we ensure a certain degree of occupation in the potentially congested routes. Results got worse when technology penetration goes down as predictions will be less accurate as a result of a 30% of vehicles not advertising their routes.

**Table 1.** Grid Scenario: average travel time

| Strategy | Average Travel Time (s) |
|---|---|
| CIwith6020 | 4717,65 |
| CIWithout6020 | 4944,8 |
| CIWithoutT10 | 4863,25 |
| CIWithoutT30 | 5307,85 |
| Basic | 5479,4 |
| NoReplanning | 10428,0 |

# 8    Conclusions and Future Work

Simulation of real-time planning and traffic coordination algorithms is an open challenge for existing traffic simulators due to both the inherent theoretical complexity of the problem and technical issues. To tackle this problem, multi agent simulators seem to be the direction to take. MATSim has shown over the last years to be one of the most proven and prominent multi agent simulators and has been successfully applied to a great variety of scenario including the traffic simulation of big cities like Zurich. Its modular architecture provides an appropriate framework for the addition of new functionality as it has been the case of *within day replanning*. Within day replanning opens the way to the simulation of en-route modification while still lacking of some needed features as support for interagent communication, modeling of network information and group formation capabilities.

In this work an extension for the MATSim simulator is presented that provides it with the previously mentioned functionalities. We show how MATSim is enabled for the simulation of real-time planning strategies once these modifications are integrated and present some preliminary results of its application in an urban scenario of low complexity. A Coordinated Anticipatory Vehicle Routing Algorithm is presented that tries to solve some of the issues found in the basic strategies. It has been shown how to apply MATSim along with the extensions which has been developed to this specially challenging scenario. Although experiments in more complex scenarios should be conducted to draw appropriate conclusions about realistic environments, we think that it could be successfully applied to bigger urban scenarios and we are conducting experiments to validate this.

# References

1. Roadmap to a single european transport area – towards a competitive and resource efficient transport system. White paper, European Commission (March 2011)
2. Abdel-Aty, M.A., Abdalla, M.F.: Examination of multiple mode/route-choice paradigms under atis. IEEE Transactions on Intelligent Transportation Systems 7(3), 332–348 (2006)
3. Ando, Y., Fukazawa, Y., Masutani, O., Iwasaki, H., Honiden, S.: Performance of pheromone model for predicting traffic congestion. In: Proceedings of the Fifth International Joint Conference on Autonomous Agents and Multiagent Systems, AAMAS 2006, pp. 73–80. ACM, New York (2006)
4. Balmer, M.: Travel demand modeling for multi-agent traffic simulations: Algorithm and systems. PhD thesis, ETH Zurich (May 2007)
5. Bazzan, A.L.C., Klügl, F.: Re-routing Agents in an Abstract Traffic Scenario. In: Zaverucha, G., da Costa, A.L. (eds.) SBIA 2008. LNCS (LNAI), vol. 5249, pp. 63–72. Springer, Heidelberg (2008)
6. Chen, B., Cheng, H.H.: A review of the applications of agent technology in traffic and transportation systems. IEEE Transactions on Intelligent Transportation Systems 11(2), 485–497 (2010)

7. Ciari, F., Balmer, M., Axhausen, K.W.: Large scale use of collective taxis. Computer applications in traffic and transportation, multi-agent systems, artificial intelligence, taxi services, transportation and traffic, ETH, Eidgenössische Technische Hochschule Zürich, IVT, Institut für Verkehrsplanung und Transportsysteme (2009)

8. Claes, R., Holvoet, T., Weyns, D.: A decentralized approach for anticipatory vehicle routing using delegate multiagent systems. IEEE Transactions on Intelligent Transportation Systems 12(2), 364–373 (2011)

9. Dobler, C.: Implementations of within day replanning in matsim-t. Technical report, ETH, Eidgenössische Technische Hochschule Zürich, IVT, Institut für Verkehrsplanung und Transportsysteme (2009)

10. Dresner, K., Stone, P.: Sharing the road: autonomous vehicles meet human drivers. In: Proceedings of the 20th International Joint Conference on Artifical Intelligence, IJCAI 2007, pp. 1263–1268. Morgan Kaufmann Publishers Inc., San Francisco (2007)

11. Ezawa, H., Mukai, N.: Adaptive Traffic Signal Control Based on Vehicle Route Sharing by Wireless Communication. In: Setchi, R., Jordanov, I., Howlett, R.J., Jain, L.C. (eds.) KES 2010, Part IV. LNCS, vol. 6279, pp. 280–289. Springer, Heidelberg (2010)

12. Fernandes, R., d'Orey, P.M., Ferreira, M.: Divert for realistic simulation of heterogeneous vehicular networks. In: 2010 IEEE 7th International Conference on Mobile Adhoc and Sensor Systems (MASS), pp. 721–726 (November 2010)

13. Hegyi, A., De Schutter, B., Hellendoorn, H.: Model predictive control for optimal coordination of ramp metering and variable speed limits. Transportation Research Part C: Emerging Technologies 13(3), 185–209 (2005)

14. Illenberger, J., Flotterod, G., Nagel, K.: Enhancing matsim with capabilities of within-day re-planning. In: Intelligent Transportation Systems Conference, ITSC 2007, September 30-October 3, pp. 94–99. IEEE (2007)

15. Kompfner, P., Reinhardt, K.: Ict for clean and efficient mobility. Final report. Technical report, eSafety Support (2008)

16. Lämmel, G., Grether, D., Nagel, K.: The representation and implementation of time-dependent inundation in large-scale microscopic evacuation simulations. Transportation Research Part C: Emerging Technologies 18(1), 84–98 (2010); Information/Communication Technologies and Travel Behaviour; Agents in Traffic and Transportation

17. Lämmer, S., Helbing, D.: Self-control of traffic lights and vehicle flows in urban road networks. Journal of Statistical Mechanics: Theory and Experiment 2008(04), P04019 (2008)

18. Nagel, K., Flötteröd, G.: Agent-based traffic assignment: going from trips to behavioral travelers. Most, 1–26 (2009)

19. Piorkowski, M., Raya, M., Lugo, A.L., Papadimitratos, P., Grossglauser, M., Hubaux, J.-P.: TraNS: Realistic Joint Traffic and Network Simulator for VANETs. ACM SIGMOBILE Mobile Computing and Communications Review (2007)

20. Rossetti, R.J.F., Bampi, S., Liu, R., Van Vliet, D., Cybis, H.B.B.: An agent-based framework for the assessment of drivers' decision making. In: 2000 IEEE Proceedings of the Intelligent Transportation Systems, pp. 387–392 (2000)

21. Sagara, H., Tanimoto, J.: A study on social diffusive impacts of a novel car-navigation-system sharing individual information in urban traffic systems. In: IEEE Congress on Evolutionary Computation, CEC 2007, pp. 836–842 (September 2007)

22. Tatomir, B., Rothkrantz, L.: Hierarchical routing in traffic using swarm-intelligence. In: Intelligent Transportation Systems Conference, ITSC 2006, pp. 230–235. IEEE (September 2006)
23. Vasirani, M., Ossowski, S.: A computational market for distributed control of urban road traffic systems. IEEE Transactions on Intelligent Transportation Systems 12(2), 313–321 (2011)
24. Vasirani, M., Ossowski, S.: A market-inspired approach to reservation-based urban road traffic management. In: Proceedings of the 8th International Conference on Autonomous Agents and Multiagent Systems, AAMAS 2009, vol. 1, pp. 617–624. International Foundation for Autonomous Agents and Multiagent Systems, Richland (2009)
25. Wahle, J., Bazzan, A.L.C., Klügl, F., Schreckenberg, M.: Decision dynamics in a traffic scenario. Physica A: Statistical Mechanics and its Applications 287(3-4), 669–681 (2000)
26. Wegener, A., Piórkowski, M., Raya, M., Hellbrück, H., Fischer, S., Hubaux, J.-P.: Traci: an interface for coupling road traffic and network simulators. In: Proceedings of the 11th Communications and Networking Simulation Symposium, CNS 2008, pp. 155–163. ACM, New York (2008)
27. Wunderlich, K.E., Kaufman, D.E., Smith, R.L.: Link travel time prediction for decentralized route guidance architectures. IEEE Transactions on Intelligent Transportation Systems 1(1), 4–14 (2000)
28. Yamashita, T., Izumi, K., Kurumatani, K., Nakashima, H.: Smooth traffic flow with a cooperative car navigation system. In: Proceedings of the Fourth International Joint Conference on Autonomous Agents and Multiagent Systems, AAMAS 2005, pp. 478–485. ACM, New York (2005)

# Agent-Based Demand Management in a Power Distribution Network by Considering Distributed Generations

Fenghui Ren[1], Minjie Zhang[1], and Danny Soetanto[2]

[1] School of Computer Science and Software Engineering
University of Wollongong, Australia
{fren,minjie}@uow.edu.au
[2] School of Electrical, Computer and Telecom Engineering
University of Wollongong, Australia
soetanto@uow.edu.au

**Abstract.** A distribution network carries electricity from transmission network to consumers through facilities such as substations, buses and feeders. Distributed generations emerge as the new alternative power resource to a distribution network at a smaller and distributed scale. On one hand, distributed generations can decrease substations' load and power price. On the other hand, they will bring difficulties to substations for demand management. This paper proposes a multiagent model to represent a radial distribution network. The model includes five types of agents, which are substation agents, bus agents, feeder agents, load agents and generation agents. Through communicating with neighbouring agents, each agent can dynamically balance its own power supply and consumption, so as to perform the demand management to the distribution network. The Java Agent Development Framework (JADE) was employed to implement the proposed agents and multiagent system. The simulation result on a case study well demonstrates the good design and performance of the proposed multiagent system in both agents communication and demand management.

**Keywords:** agent-based modelling, power distribution network, distributed generation.

## 1 Introduction

In a power system, the distribution network carries electricity from the transmission network and delivers electricity to consumers. In Australia, the distribution network starts from secondary substations, which reduce the voltage from 33/66KV to 11/22KV, and deliver electricity to local transformers through *Medium Voltage* (MV) feeders. Then the local transformers further reduce the voltage to 240/415V, and deliver power to residential or commercial consumers through *Low Voltage* (LV) feeders. In Figure 1, an example of the distribution network is illustrated. Typically, the distribution network would contain facilities such as substations, buses, feeders and loads. In a traditional distribution network, the power is strictly delivered from upstream facilities to downstream facilities. The secondary substation centrally monitors the loads in a distribution network, and performs the demand management.

S. Cranefield and I. Song (Eds.): PRIMA 2011 Workshops, LNAI 7580, pp. 109–124, 2012.
© Springer-Verlag Berlin Heidelberg 2012

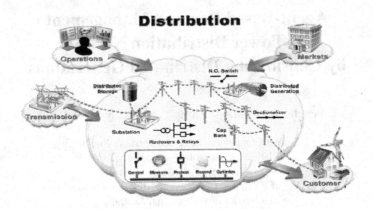

**Fig. 1.** An overview of the distribution network

Distributed Generation (DG) emerges as a new alternative power resource to a distribution network at a smaller and distributed scale. The appearance of DGs takes both advantages and disadvantages to the distribution network. On one hand, DGs can connects to LV feeders directly and supply power to the network near the loads without going through the secondary substation and the transmission network, which will significantly decrease the power loss in transmission and share the power loads between Bulk Generations (BG). On the other hand, most DGs can only provide intermittent power and the secondary substations usually lack of information about the DGs, which will cause problems in demand management. Furthermore, the power flow may become not strict from the upstream to the downstream, but may dynamically change according to the DGs' supply and customers' consumption. How to dynamically perform the demand management and efficiently balance the demand and supply in the distribution network by considering the DGs becomes a challenging research issue in power engineering.

In order to efficiently manage and control the power network, Multi-Agent Systems (MASs) have been employed to solve the challenges in power network, and are being developed for a range of applications including fault diagnostics, system monitoring, system restoration, system simulation, and system control [1] [5] [10]. Nagata et al. proposed a multi-agent approach for decentralized power system restoration in a distribution system network [7] [6]. The *load agent* collects information about the power system, and the *feeder agent* controls the entire restoration process in accordance with the priority in the restoration strategy. Lin et al. proposed a centralized multi-agent system to model the power distribution between substations and end-users [4]. The distribution feeders and substation transformers are modeled by FCB agent and MTR agent, respectively. Nordman and Lehtonen presented their agent concepts for managing electrical distribution networks by using decentralized functionality [8] [9]. The distribution automation applications are executed by local substation controllers through collaboration with neighboring substations. Solanki et al. presented a decentralized solution for distribution power system restoration [11]. Agents have the abilities to communicate and collaborate with other agents to perform individual or group tasks. Kodama et al.

proposed an autonomous restoration approach for power distribution network by using the Contract Net Protocol [3]. An agent in the outage area will broadcast a connection task in the network, and all valid agents in the generation area will bid for that. The agent in the outage area will decide which generation area the agent should fulfill the task based on its interests.

In this paper, we propose a fully decentralized Multiagent System (MAS) to model the distribution network and DGs. The MAS contains five types of agents, i.e., Substation Agent (SA), Bus Agent (BA), Feeder Agent (FA), Generation Agent (GA), and Load Agent (LA). Agents can only communicate with the neighbouring agents, and dynamically balance the supply and consumption by considering the network's situations and their own capacities. The organization of this paper is as follows. Section 2 introduces the principle of the proposed MAS. Section 3 introduces how the proposed MAS is implemented. Section 4 introduces a case study in a distribution network and illustrates the simulation result by JADE. Section 5 concludes this paper and also mentions our future work.

## 2   The Principle of the Proposed Multiagent System

In this section, we introduce the principle of the proposed MAS for demand management in the distribution network. The purposes of the MAS are to (i) dynamically balance the power supply and demand in the distribution network; (ii) maximise the usage of the power from DGs; and (iii) minimise the cost on power usage. We have two assumptions about the distribution network: (i) the unit electricity price from a DG is lower than the unit electricity price from a secondary substation; and (ii) the distribution network supports bi-direction power flow and redundant power can be sent back to the primary substations through the secondary substations.

### 2.1   Objectives and Restrictions

In this subsection, we firstly introduce the mathematical objectives and restrictions of the proposed MAS. The objectives include *Balance Objective* and *Cost Objective*, and the restrictions include *Line Restriction* and *Capacity Restriction*. For a facility $i$ (i.e., a substation, a generation, a bus, a feeder, or a load) in a distribution network, let $p_i^+$ be the power generated by $i$ and $c_i^+$ be the price by generating an unit power. Let $p_{i \to j}$ be the power delivered from $i$ to $j$ and $c_{i \to j}$ be the price by delivering an unit power from $i$ to $j$. Let $p_i^-$ be the power consumed by $i$ and $c_i^-$ be the price by consuming an unit power. The objectives and restrictions are introduced as follows.

**Balance Objective:** For each facility $i$ in the distribution network, we must ensure the power delivering to and from $i$ are balanced, i.e.,

$$p_i^+ + \sum_{j \in J^+} p_{j \to i} = p_i^- + \sum_{k \in J^-} p_{i \to k} \tag{1}$$

where $J^+$ indicates $i$'s neighbouring facilities which deliver power to $i$, and $J^-$ indicates $i$'s neighbouring facilities which get power from $i$.

*Balance Objective* is our first objective, it is a very important considerations in power management. It ensures the balance of the distribution network on power supply and demand. Equation 1 specifies that the power generated by a facility plus the power delivered from all its neighbouring facilities should always equal to the power consumed by the facility plus the power delivered to all its neighbouring facilities.

**Cost Objective:** For each facility $i$ in the distribution network, we want minimise its cost on power consuming and delivering. facility $i$'s cost on an unit power is defined as follows:

$$c_i^- = \frac{p_i^+ \times c_i^+ + \sum_{j \in J+} p_{j \to i} \times c_{j \to i}}{p_i^+ + \sum_{j \in J+} p_{j \to i}} \quad (2)$$

and $i$'s spending on delivering an unit power to facility $k$ is:

$$c_{i \to k} = c_i^- + c_{i,k}^{line} \quad (3)$$

where $c_{i,k}^{line}$ is the cost on the physical line from facilities $i$ to $k$. Because we already assume that the distribution network supports bi-direction power flow, so $c_{i,k}^{line} = c_{k,i}^{line}$.

*Cost Objective* is the second objective, and it considers the economy issue in power management. It ensures that the cost on power consuming and delivering is minimised. Because we already assumed that the power price from DGs is lower than the power price from bulk generations, so *Cost Objective* can also ensure that the power generated by DGs is consumed firstly in the distribution network.

**Line Restriction:** For each physical line connecting facilities $i$ and $k$, i.e., $line_{i,k}$, the electric current from $i$ to $k$ should be no greater than the line's limitation, i.e.,

$$I_{i \to k} \leq I_{i,k}^{lim} \quad (4)$$

where $I_{i \to k}$ is the current from $i$ to $k$, and $I_{i,j}^{lim}$ is maximum current that $line_{i,j}$ allows. Because we already assume that the distribution network supports bi-direction power flow, so $I_{i,k}^{lim} = I_{k,i}^{lim}$.

*Line Restriction* is one of the significant issues in the real-world distribution network, and will affect how power is delivered from the substation to the consumer. The purpose of *Line Restriction* is to protect the physical cable in-between facilities.

**Capacity Restriction:** For each facility $i$ in the distribution network, its capacies in power generating and/or consuming definitely have limitations. Also, each facility has a limitation on the electric current. Therefore, the restrictions on power generating and/or consuming are defined as follows:

$$p_i^+ \leq p_i^{+lim} \quad (5)$$

and,

$$p_i^- \leq p_i^{-lim} \quad (6)$$

where $p_i^+$ and $p_i^-$ are the power generated and/or consumed by $i$, and $p_i^{+lim}$ and $p_i^{-lim}$ are the limitations on power generating and/or consuming for $i$.

The limitation on the electric current for facility $i$ is defined as following:

$$I_i^+ + \sum_{j \in J+} I_{j \to i} \leq I_i^{+lim} \tag{7}$$

where $I_i^+$ is the current generated by $i$, $I_{j \to i}$ is the current from $j$ to $i$, and $I_i^{+lim}$ is $i$'s input current limitation. Similarly, we have

$$I_i^- + \sum_{k \in J-} I_{i \to k} \leq I_i^{-lim} \tag{8}$$

where $I_i^-$ is the current consumed by $i$, $I_{i \to k}$ is the current from $i$ to $k$, and $I_i^{-lim}$ is $i$'s output current limitation. In the distribution network which supports bi-direction current flow, $I_i^{+lim} = I_i^{-lim}$.

*Capacity Restriction* is another significant issue that should be considered in the real-world distribution network. It will affect the power resource selection and power allocation in the distribution network. Equations 5-8 indicate the power and the current go through a facility should no greater than its limitation. The purpose of *Capacity Restriction* is to protect the facilities in a distribution network.

## 2.2 System Organisation

This subsection introduces how the MAS is organised. We proposed five types of agent, which are *substation agent* (SA), *bus agent* (BA), *feeder agent* (FA), *load agent* (LA), and *generation agent* (GA). Basically, the proposed MAS employs decentralised structure and agents can only communicate with their neighbouring agents. The communication between nonadjacent agents is fulfilled through the messages forwarding through other agents in-between them. Through exchanging information with the neighbouring agents, each agent can dynamically collect information about its local area, and balance its power demand and supply by using the local information. Consequently, the systemic balance will also be achieved through the contribution of each individual agent. In general, the proposed MAS has three merits by comparison with traditional distribution network system, which are (i) the proposed MAS supports communication between neighbouring agents, and information can be delivered among agents; (ii) the proposed MAS can dynamically balance the power demand and supply through using only local information; and (iii) the proposed MAS is robust and extendable in different system scales. Agents play as a "plug and operate" component, and can easily connect to or disconnect from the system. In the following paragraphs, the functionality and the rule for each proposed agent is introduced.

**Substation Agent (SA)**
*Functionality (i):* Connect/disconnect to the MAS
*Rule:* A SA can be connect or disconnect to a BA in the MAS. Once the SA is connected to a BA, it will exchange information with the BA, and create a record for the BA. The record includes information about the BA's power supply capacity, power supply cost,

and power consumption capacity. Also the line information between the SA and the BA is recorded.

*Functionality (ii):* Exchange information between neighbouring agents
*Rule:* Once the SA receives updated information from a BA or from an upstream facility, the SA will update its record about the BA or the facility, and forward the information to other neighbouring agents.

*Functionality (iii):* Adjust power supply and consumption
*Rule:* If more power are required by a neighbouring agent, the SA will check its supply capacity and the physical line's limitation to decide whether the additional power can be supplied. In case the distribution network has redundant power, the SA will check its consumption capacity and the line's limitation, and delivers power to its upstream facility, i.e., the primary substation.

## Bus Agent (BA)
*Functionality (i):* Connect/disconnet to the MAS
*Rule:* A BA can be connected to any type of agents in the MAS. After been connected, the BA will send its information, such as capacity, to all neighbours, and also record all neighbouring agent's information.

*Functionality (ii):* Exchange information between neighbouring agents
*Rule:* Once a BA receives updated information about power supply cost from a neighbouring agent, the BA will recalculate its power supply cost and forward the cost information to the neighbouring agents who get power from the BA. Once the BA receives updated information about capacity from a neighbouring agent, the BA will update its record and forward the information to other neighbouring agents.

*Functionality (iii):* Re-select power resources
*Rule:* If a BA's power supply cost changes, the BA will re-select the power resources from its neighbouring agents in order to minimising its power supply cost. If a BA's neighbouring agent asks for more power, the BA will try to select suitable resources by considering both cost and restrictions. If a BA has redundant power, the BA will contact its upstream agent and deliver the extra power to its upstream facility.

## Feeder Agent (FA)
*Functionality (i):* Connect/disconnet to the MAS
*Rule:* A FA can be connected only to a BA. After been connected, the FA will exchange its information with its neighbouring BAs.

*Functionality (ii):* Exchange information between neighbouring BAs
*Rule:* Once a FA receives updated information from its upstream or downstream BAs, the FA will update its record about the corresponding BAs, and further forward the information to its downstream or upstream BAs.

*Functionality (iii):* Change power flow direction
*Rule:* If a FA's neighbouring BAs change their demand on power, the power flow direction may changed as well. The FA will monitor such a change and adapt the power flow direction immediately.

### Load Agent (LA)
*Functionality (i):* Connect/disconnet to the MAS
*Rule:* A LA can only be connected to a BA. After been connected, the LA will inform the BA its consumption capacity and get the supply capacity from the BA.

*Functionality (ii):* Adjust power consumed
*Rule:* If a LA needs more power from its upstream BA or want to decrease its load, the LA will submit a request to the BA and waits for the response. Once the request is approved, the LA will perform a consequent action.

### Generation Agent (GA)
*Functionality (i):* Connect/disconnet to the MAS
*Rule:* A GA can only be connected to a BA. After been connected, the GA will inform the BA its supply capacity and get the consumption capacity from the BA.

*Functionality (ii):* Adjust power supplied
*Rule:* If a GA wants to increase or decrease its power supply to its upstream BA, the LA will submit an request to the BA and waits for the response. Once the request is approved, the LA will perform a consequent action.

In Figure 2, we display an example of radial distribution network. The number associated with a line indicates the power transferred by the line, and the arrow indicates the direction of the power. This distribution network contains one substation, nine buses, four feeders, eight loads, and three distributed generations. By employing the proposed MAS, this radial distribution network is represented in Figure 3.

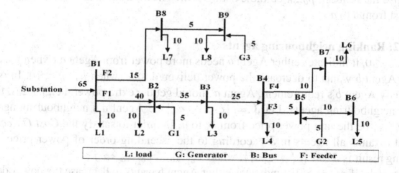

**Fig. 2.** An example of distribution network

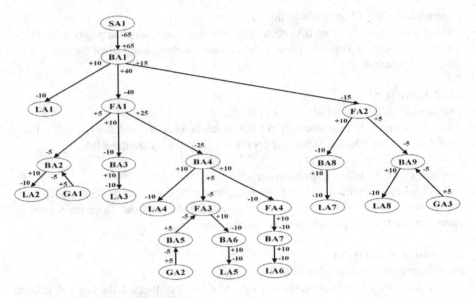

**Fig. 3.** Agent-based modelling on the distribution network

## 2.3  Demand Management

In the proposed MAS, LAs can adapt their power consumptions, and both SAs and GAs can adapt their power supply. The BA and FA will perform demand management to dynamically balance the supply and consumption between LAs, SAs and GAs. Basically, the demand management contains four steps.

### Step 1: Receiving requests

The demand management process starts when a BA or a FA receives a request from a neighbouring agent. Let $a$ be the BA or the FA, $b$ be the neighbouring agent who initialise the request, $p_{a \to b}$ be the existing power flows from $a$ to $b$, and $r_{b \to a}$ be the request from $b$ to $a$.

### Step 2: Ranking neighbouring agents

If $r_{b \to a} < 0$, it indicates either Agent $b$ needs more power from Agent $a$ (when $p_{a \to b} \geq 0$) or Agent $b$ wants to decrease the power delivered to $a$ (when $p_{a \to b} < 0$). In order to satisfy Agent $b$'s requirement, Agent $a$ should get the extra power, i.e., $|r_{b \to a}|$, from other neighbouring agents. Let $\mathbf{J} = \{c_1, \ldots, c_J\}$ be Agent $a$'s neighbouring agents, and $c_{c_j \to a}$ be the unit power price from $c_j$ to $a$. In order to satisfy the *Cost Objective*, Agent $a$ ranks all agents in $\mathbf{J}$ according to the ascending order of power price. The ranking result is $\mathbf{J^a} = \{c_1^a, \ldots, c_J^a\}$, where $c_{c_j^a \to a} \leq c_{c_k^a \to a} \Leftrightarrow j \leq k$.

Similarly, if $r_{b \to a} \geq 0$, it indicates either Agent $b$ wants to decrease the power delivered from Agent $a$ (when $p_{a \to b} \geq 0$) or Agent $b$ wants to increase the power delivered to $a$ (when $p_{a \to b} < 0$). In order to satisfy Agent $b$'s requirement, Agent $a$ should find neighbouring agents to consume the extra power, i.e., $|r_{b \to a}|$. Let $\mathbf{J^d} = \{c_1^d, \ldots, c_J^d\}$

be the ranking of $\mathbf{J}$ according to the descending order of power price, then $c_{c_j^d \rightarrow a} \geq c_{c_k^d \rightarrow a} \Leftrightarrow j \leq k$.

After Agent $a$ ranks its neighbouring agents, Agent $a$ will contact them orderly. Let $c_j$ be the next agent from $\mathbf{J^a}$ (when $r_{b \rightarrow a} < 0$) or from $\mathbf{J^d}$ (when $r_{b \rightarrow a} \geq 0$), then Agent $a$ will enter next step.

**Step 3: Forwarding requests and selecting resources**
Let $p_{c_j \rightarrow a}$ be the existing power flowing from $c_j$ to $a$, and $p_{c_j}^{+lim}$ be Agent $c_j$'s limitation on power supply. Then $r_{a \rightarrow c_j} = \min(p_{c_j}^{+lim} - p_{c_j \rightarrow a}, |r_{b \rightarrow a}|)$ is the request from Agent $a$ to Agent $c_j$ on power. Agent $a$ will send its request $r_{a \rightarrow c_j}$ to Agent $c_j$.

If Agent $c_j$ is a BA or a FA, then Agent $c_j$ will starts another demand management process within its neighbouring agents to decide whether Agent $a$'s request can be satisfied. If Agent $c_j$ is a SA, a GA, or a LA, it will generate response to Agent $a$ straightway according to its capacity on power supply and/or consumption. Let $\tilde{r}_{a \rightarrow c_j}$ be Agent $c_j$'s response, and $r'_{b \rightarrow a} = r_{b \rightarrow a} - \tilde{r}_{a \rightarrow c_j}$ be the remaining of Agent $b$'s request on power. If $r'_{b \rightarrow a} > 0$, it indicates that more power requirements should be allocated, and Agent $a$ will pick up the next neighbouring agent from its ranking list, and repeat Step 3. Such a procedure is repeated until $r'_{b \rightarrow a} = 0$ or Agent $a$'s ranking list becomes empty.

**Step 4: Replying requests and updating information**
If Step 3 is completed with $r'_{b \rightarrow a} = 0$, Agent $a$ will reply Agent $b$ $\tilde{r}_{b \rightarrow a} = r_{b \rightarrow a}$ to indicate Agent $b$'s request is fully satisfied. Otherwise, Agent $a$ will reply Agent $b$ $\tilde{r}_{b \rightarrow a} = r_{b \rightarrow a} - r'_{b \rightarrow a}$ to indicate Agent $b$'s request is partially satisfied. Finally, Agent $a$ updates its information about neighbouring agents' power supply/consumption and power price, and further forwards self's updating to other neighbouring agents.

Taking the distribution network in Figure 2 as an example, if Load L8 requests to increase its load from $10MW$ to $20MW$, and Generation G3's limitation on power supply is $10MW$, then the demand management procedure is illustrated in Figure 4. The procedure contains 10 steps, which are: (i) LA8 requests extra $10MW$ power from BA9; (ii) BA9 requests more $5MW$ power from GA3; (iii) GA3 agrees to supply more $5MW$ to BA9's; (iv) BA9 requests more $5MW$ from FA2; (v) FA2 forwards the request to BA1; (vi) BA1 further forwards the request to SA1; (vii) SA1 agrees to supply more $5MW$ to BA1; (viii) BA1 agrees to supply more $5MW$ to FA2; (ix) FA2 agrees to supply more $5MW$ to BA9; and (x) BA9 agrees to supply more $10MW$ to LA8. After the procedure completes, the updated distribution network is displayed in Figure 5.

# 3   Agent Development

We employ the Java Agent Development Framework (JADE) to implement the proposed agents. Basically, JADE, implemented in Java, is a middleware for the development and run-time execution of peer-to-peer applications that use agents. In JADE, the local name of the agent is converted into globally unique Agent ID (AID) automatically. The

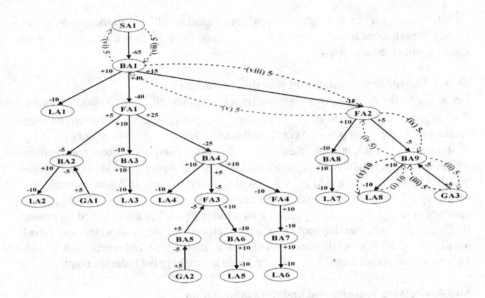

**Fig. 4.** An example of agent-based demand management

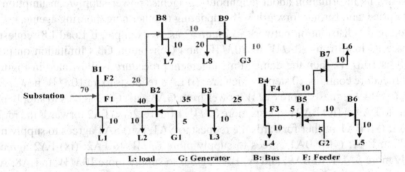

**Fig. 5.** The distribution network after demand management

communication among agents in JADE is carried out according to FIPA-specified Agent Communication Language (ACL) [2]. Agents communicate by asynchronous message passing using some predefined so-called performative of message such as: REQUEST, INFORM, REFUSE and AGREE. ACL message passed between agents are characterized by (i) performative, (ii) conversation ID, (iii) sender, (iv) intended receiver, and (v) content. The communicate content used in the proposed MAS is defined by the ontologies in Table 1. We totally define five concept ontology (i.e., *Power, Cost, Limit, Line* and *Neighbour*) and four action ontology (i.e., *Connect/Disconnect, Update-Cost, Update-Limit*, and *Change-Power*). The concept ontology were used by agents to describe a concept or the status of components and cables in a distribution network, and the action ontology were used to indicate agents' actions. Table 2 shows the *performative, conversation ID, sender*, and *intended receiver* for agents' behaviours, where the *performative* is the predefined keywords to indicate the communication purpose, the *conversation ID* indicates the unique identification of a conversation, the *sender* is the agent who initiates the conversation, and the *receiver* is the agent who should response the *sender*'s requests.

**Table 1.** Ontology for agent communication

| Ontology Name | Ontology Type | Slot Name | Slot Type | Mandatory/Optional |
|---|---|---|---|---|
| Power | Concept | from-power | Float | Mandatory |
| | | to-power | Float | Mandatory |
| Cost | Concept | from-cost | Float | Mandatory |
| | | to-cost | Float | Mandatory |
| Limitation | Concept | limit-power | Power Ontology | Mandatory |
| Line | Concept | id | String | Mandatory |
| | | limitation | Limitation Ontology | Mandatory |
| | | power | Power Ontology | Mandatory |
| | | cost | Float | Mandatory |
| Neighbour | Concept | name | String | Mandatory |
| | | type | String | Mandatory |
| | | level | String | Optional |
| | | line | Line Ontology | Optional |
| | | cost | Cost Ontology | Mandatory |
| | | limit | limitation Ontology | Mandatory |
| Connect | Action | type | String | Mandatory |
| | | level | String | Mandatory |
| | | line | Line Ontology | Mandatory |
| | | cost | Cost Ontology | Mandatory |
| | | limit | limitation Ontology | Mandatory |
| Update-Cost | Action | cost | Cost Ontology | Mandatory |
| Update-Limitation | Action | limit | Limitation Ontology | Mandatory |
| Change-Power | Action | change | Float | Mandatory |
| | | cost | Float | Mandatory |

**Table 2.** Description of behaviours associated with agents

| Agents | Behaviours | Send Message | Receive Message | Description |
|---|---|---|---|---|
| Facility Agent (including Bus Agent and Feeder Agent) | ConnectParent | performative "REQUEST", conversation ID "connect-parent", sender "Downstream agent", receiver "Upstream agent", content "(type, 'child', line, cost, limit)" | performative "AGREE/REFUSE", conversation ID "connect-parent", sender "Upstream agent", receiver "Downstream agent", content "(type, 'parent', line, cost, limit)" | Sends message to an upstream agent for connection purpose; receives "AGREE/REFUSE" for a successful/unsuccessful result; exchanges information in predefined format. |
| | ChangePower | performative "REQUEST", conversation ID "change-power", sender "Neighbour agent", receiver "Neighbour agent", content "(power, cost)" | performative "AGREE/REFUSE", conversation ID "change-power", sender "Neighbour agent", receiver "Neighbour agent", content "(power, cost)" | Sends message to an neighbouring agent to adjust power supply/consumption; receives "AGREE/REFUSE" for a successful/unsuccessful result; receives the actual power and power price. |
| | UpdateCost | performative "INFORM", conversation ID "update-cost", sender "Neighbour agent", receiver "Neighbour agent", content "(cost)" | performative "INFORM", conversation ID "update-cost", sender "Neighbour agent", receiver "Neighbour agent", content "(cost)" | Sends message to neighbouring agents to informing changes of power price; receives power price change from a neighbouring agent; forwards power price change information to other neighbouring agents. |
| | UpdateLimitation | performative "INFORM", conversation ID "update-limit", sender "Neighbour agent", receiver "Neighbour agent", content "(limitation)" | performative "INFORM", conversation ID "update-limit", sender "Neighbour agent", receiver "Neighbour agent", content "(limitation)" | Sends message to neighbouring agents to informing changes of limitation on power supply/consumption; receives limitation change from a neighbouring agent; forwards limitation change information to other neighbouring agents. |
| Substation Agent | ChangePower | performative "AGREE/REFUSE", conversation ID "change-power", sender "a SA", receiver "a BA", content "(power, cost)" | performative "REQUEST", conversation ID "change-power", sender "a BA", receiver "a SA", content "(power, cost)" | receives change power "REQUEST" from a BA; replies 'AGREE' if can fully satisfy the requirement and "REFUSE" if can not fully satisfy the requirement; replies actual power and power price. |
| Generation Agent | ChangePower | performative "AGREE/REFUSE", conversation ID "change-power", sender "a GA", receiver "a BA", content "(power, cost)" | performative "REQUEST", conversation ID "change-power", sender "a BA", receiver "a GA", content "(power, cost)" | receives change power "REQUEST" from a BA; replies "AGREE" if can fully supply the required power and "REFUSE" if can not fully supply the required power; replies actual power and power price. |
| Load Agent | ChangePower | performative "REQUEST", conversation ID "change-power", sender "a LA", receiver "a BA", content "(power, cost)" | performative "AGREE/REFUSE", conversation ID "change-power", sender "a BA", receiver "a CA", content "(power, cost)" | Sends message to a BA to adjust power consumption; receives "AGREE/REFUSE" for a successful/unsuccessful result; receives the actual power and power price. |

## 4   Case Study

In this section, we show the performance of the proposed MAS through a case study. In Figure 6(a), a distribution network is illustrated, which contains one substation, three buses, two feeders, two distributed generations, and one load. The capacity for substation, bus and feeder is set in-between $(-50MW, 50MW)$ (a positive value indicating the current flows from an upstream facility to a downstream facility, and a negative value indicates an adverse power flow). The maximum power supply ability for all distributed generations is $10MW$, and maximum power consumption ability for loads is $20MW$. Figure 6(a) shows the moment when the two distribution generations provide power to the load, and there is no power delivered from the substation to the distribution network. In order to change the power consumption in the distribution network, we assume that another load, i.e., L2, connects to the distribution network. After L2 is connected, because more power is needed, the substation will supply the extra power to the distribution network. The updated distribution network is illustrated in Figure 6(b).

We use the proposed MAS to simulate the above process. Firstly, Figure 7(a) simulate the moment before LA2 is connected. It can be seen that GA1 supplies $10MW$ power to LA1 through BA2, and GA1 also supplies $10MW$ power to LA1 through the path $GA2 \rightarrow BA3 \rightarrow FA2 \rightarrow BA1 \rightarrow FA1 \rightarrow BA2 \rightarrow LA1$. No power is delivered to the distribution network from SA1. Secondly, Figure 7(b) illustrates the communications among agents when LA2 requests to connect the distribution network and asks for $20MW$ after connection. In Table 3, we explain such a process in details based on the communication sequence displayed in Figure 7(b), and illustrate the procedure (from "Communication 11") in Figure 8. Finally, Figure 7(c) displays the distribution network after LA2 was connected. It can be seen that $20MW$ more power was delivered from SA1 to the distribution network, and the power price for each agent is also updated correspondingly. The simulation of such a case study well demonstrates the good performance of the proposed MAS in both agents communication and demand management.

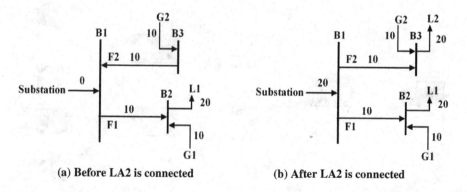

(a) Before LA2 is connected              (b) After LA2 is connected

**Fig. 6.** A case study

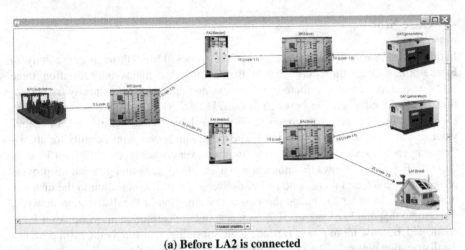

(a) Before LA2 is connected

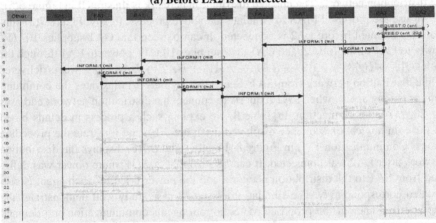

(b) The communications among agents when LA2 is connected

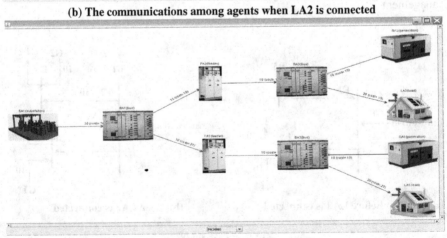

(c) After LA2 is connected

**Fig. 7.** Simulation result of the case study

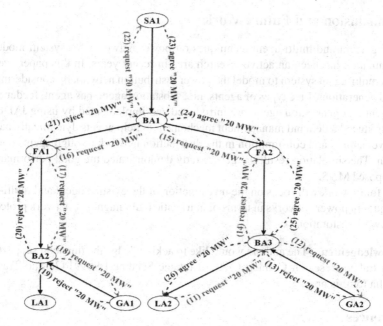

**Fig. 8.** The communication between agents

**Table 3.** Explanation of Figure 7(b)

| Communication Order | Explanation |
|---|---|
| 1 | LA2 requests to connect BA3. |
| 2 | BA3 agrees LA2 to connect. |
| 3 - 10 | BA3 informs FA2 that BA3's consumption capacity was changed. Then such a change is further forwarded to other agents in the MAS. Each agent updates its knowledge about neighbouring agents' consumption capacity. |
| 11 | LA2 requests $20MW$ from BA3. |
| 12 - 13 | BA3 firstly requests $20MW$ more power from GA2 (to maximise local power utilise). However, because GA2 already reached its maximum power supply, GA2 refuses BA3's request. |
| 14 - 15 | Then BA3 requests more $20MW$ from FA2, and FA2 forwards the request to BA1. |
| 16 - 21 | BA1 firstly requests more $20MW$ from FA1 (to maximise the usage of local power), then FA1 forwards the request to BA2, then BA2 further forwards the request to GA1. Because GA1 already reached its maximum power supply, GA1 refuses BA2's request. Therefore, BA2 refuses FA1's request and FA1 refuses the original request from BA1. |
| 22 - 23 | Then BA1 requests more $20MW$ from SA1, and SA1 agrees BA1's request. |
| 24 - 25 | Consequently, BA1 replies FA2 with an agreement, and FA2 forwards such an agreement to BA3. |
| 26 | Finally, BA3 finds enough power to fully satisfy LA2's request, and agrees LA2 to supply the $20MW$ power. |

# 5   Conclusion and Future Work

Applying agent and multi-agent techniques on power networks for system modelling and simulation has been an active research area in recent years. In this paper, we proposed a multi-agent system to model the power distribution network by considering distributed generations. Five types of agents, i.e., substation agent, bus agent, feeder agent, load agent and generation agent, are introduced and implemented by using JADE. We also introduced a demand management mechanism to help agents dynamically balance the power supply and consumption in the distribution network through agents communication. The simulation result on a case study demonstrated the good performance of the proposed MAS.

Our future work will focus on the investigation of the existing agent and multi-agent techniques in power networks in terms of automatic fault diagnosis, network protection, and network restoration.

**Acknowledgement.** The authors would like to acknowledge the financial support from the Australian Research Council (ARC) Linkage Scheme LP0991428 and Transgrid Australia for this project.

# References

1. Baran, M., El-Markabi, I.: A Multiagent-based Dispatching Scheme for Distributed Generators for Voltage Support on Distribution Feeders. IEEE Transactions on Power Systems 22(1), 52–59 (2007)
2. Bellifemine, F., Caire, G., Greenwood, D.: Developing Multi-Agent Systems with JADE, vol. 5. Wiley (2007)
3. Kodama, J., Hamagami, T., Shinji, H., Tanabe, T., Funabashi, T., Hirata, H.: Multi-agent-based Autonomous Power Distribution Network Restoration Using Contract Net Protocol. Electrical Engineering in Japan 166(4), 56–63 (2009)
4. Lin, C., Chen, C., Ku, T., Tsai, C., Ho, C.: A Multiagent-Based Distribution Automation System for Service Restoration of Fault Contingencies. European Transactions on Electrical Power 21(1), 239–253 (2011)
5. McArthur, S., Davidson, E., Catterson, V., Dimeas, A., Hatziargyriou, N., Ponci, F., Funabashi, T.: Multi-Agent Systems for Power Engineering Applications–Part I: Concepts, Approaches, and Technical Challenges. IEEE Transactions on Power Systems 22(4), 1743–1752 (2007)
6. Nagata, T., Fujita, H., Sasaki, H.: Decentralized Approach to Normal Operations for Power System Network. In: 13th Int. Conf. on Intelligent Systems Application to Power Systems, pp. 407–412 (2005)
7. Nagata, T., Tao, Y., Sasaki, H., Fujita, H.: A Multiagent Approach to Distribution System Restoration. Electrical Engineering in Japan 152(3), 21–28 (2005)
8. Nordman, M., Lehtonen, M.: An Agent Concept for Managing Electrical Distribution Networks. IEEE Transactions on Power Delivery 20(2 Part 1), 696–703 (2005)
9. Nordman, M., Lehtonen, M.: Distributed Agent-Based State Estimation for Electrical Distribution Networks. IEEE Transactions on Power Systems 20(2), 652–658 (2005)
10. Pipattanasomporn, M., Feroze, H., Rahman, S.: Multi-Agent Systems in A Distributed Smart Grid: Design and implementation. In: Power Systems Conference and Exposition, pp. 1–8 (2009)
11. Solanki, J., Khushalani, S., Schulz, N.: A Multi-Agent Solution to Distribution Systems Restoration. IEEE Transactions on Power Systems 22(3), 1026–1034 (2007)

# Author Index